A ROYAL·
CHRISTMAS

Christmas and New Year Good Wishes

A ROYAL · CHRISTMAS

Louise Cooling

ROYAL COLLECTION TRUST

CONTENTS

INTRODUCTION

HROUGH A THOUSAND YEARS OF BRITISH HISTORY, SINCE THE CORONATION OF WILLIAM THE CONQUEROR (1028–87) ON CHRISTMAS DAY 1066, THE CELEBRATION OF CHRISTMAS AND THE FESTIVE SEASON HAS BEEN ONE OF THE MOST IMPORTANT EVENTS IN THE ROYAL CALENDAR.

Over the centuries, kings and queens have celebrated Christmas in many ways. In the Middle Ages, medieval monarchs presided over immense feasts in the Great Halls of Westminster and Woodstock, where guests dined on gilded peacock, roast swan and wild boar's head. At the Tudor and Stuart courts, solemn religious services were followed by elaborate pageants and masques, led by the Lord of Misrule, in which the king and queen often took part. In the eighteenth and nineteenth centuries, Queen Victoria (1819–1901) and her Hanoverian predecessors enjoyed altogether more domestic Christmases at favourite royal residences including Windsor, Brighton and Osborne, where

This happy, most blessed Festival again returns, & with it so many joyful feelings.
— QUEEN VICTORIA, 24 DECEMBER 1846

Henrik Emanuel
Wigström (1862–
1923) for Fabergé,
Holly sprig, c.1908,
RCIN 40501

celebrations centred on the exchange of gifts and
family activities. Since the start of the twentieth
century, the monarch's Christmas has been a private
family occasion, principally spent at the favoured
royal retreat of Sandringham in Norfolk, where many
of the traditions established by Queen Victoria and
Prince Albert (1819–61) are still alive.

Throughout the ages, the festive celebrations of
kings, queens, the royal family and the court have
influenced many of the Christmas customs now
enjoyed yearly by countless people around the world.
From the first appearance of turkey on the festive
feast table of Henry VIII (1491–1547) in the 1540s,
to the introduction of the Christmas tree to Britain by
Queen Charlotte (1744–1818) in the late eighteenth
century, the monarchy has helped to popularise many
of the most treasured festive traditions.

Today, with the institution of the Christmas broadcast
by her grandfather King George V (1865–1936) in 1932,
Her Majesty Queen Elizabeth II (b.1952) herself now plays an
important part in Christmas Day for many millions of people in
Britain and the Commonwealth.

CEREMONIES
& TRADITIONS

A S WELL AS BEING THE SEASON
OF CELEBRATION, FEASTING
AND GIFT GIVING, CHRISTMAS
HAS ALWAYS BEEN A TIME FOR SOLEMN
RELIGIOUS OBSERVANCES AT COURT.

*The return of this blessed season
must always fill one with
gratitude & with the deepest
devotion to our Lord & Saviour!*

QUEEN VICTORIA,
25 DECEMBER 1850

Since the time of William the Conqueror, it has
been traditional for the sovereign and the royal
family to go to church on Christmas Day morning. Historically,
Christmas Day was one of the few occasions when the monarch
would wear a crown to attend a church service. By the reign of
Charles II (1630–85) Christmas Day was also one of the 12 'collar
days', when the monarch would make an offering on the high altar.
Other 'collar days', so called because the collars of various orders of
knighthood are worn, include New Year's Day, Epiphany and Easter,
and are still part of the court calendar today.

On Christmas Day in the reign of Henry VIII, the King would
hear Mass in private in his Closet before going in procession to the
Chapel Royal for Matins. In 1551 Edward VI (1537–53) issued the

HM Queen Elizabeth II and other members of the Royal Family leave St George's Chapel, Windsor on Christmas Day, 1978.

Holy Days and Fasting Days Act, which declared that all subjects had to attend church services held on Christmas Day. Additionally, services were to be attended on the Feast of Circumcision of Christ, traditionally celebrated on New Year's Day in the Anglican Church, and on the Feast of the Epiphany on 6 January, which marked the close of the festive season.

For centuries, it was traditional for the monarch and their family to attend the service on Christmas morning in one of the private royal chapels. Describing an otherwise uneventful Christmas Day in 1793, Queen Charlotte, the wife of George III (1738–1820), noted that the royal family attended Matins in the King's Chapel at Windsor Castle and received the sacrament.

For Queen Victoria, while Christmas was a great family occasion full of feasting and entertainment, it was also a time for religious observance and thanksgiving. On Christmas Eve 1843, the Queen noted in her journal:

'This happy day has again returned, & it seems but yesterday we had last celebrated it. Time flies too fast. I feel certain that our Heavenly Father through His blessed Son, whose birth we at this time so joyfully & gratefully commemorate, will grant that we may celebrate many more happy Christmas Eves together, & with our Children.'

On Christmas Day five years later, Queen Victoria described how, following the morning church service, she 'Talked to Vicky [Victoria, Princess Royal (1840–1901)] & Bertie [Albert Edward, Prince of Wales (1841–1910)] together of this day, the meaning of the great festival, & read to them part of the account of the birth of Our Saviour'. In 1900, towards the end of her life, Queen Victoria

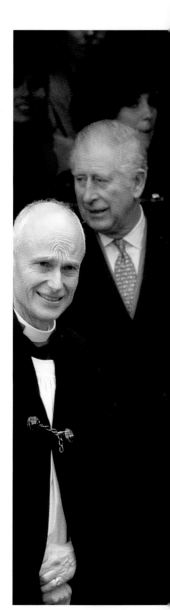

The Royal Family attending St Mary Magdalene Church, Sandringham, on Christmas Day, 2017

was too frail to attend the church service on
Christmas morning, so in the afternoon a short
service was held in one of the drawing rooms at
Osborne House.

Today, The Queen and other members of
the Royal Family attend the morning service
on Christmas Day at St Mary Magdalene,
Sandringham, a sixteenth-century country
church once visited by The Queen's great-
great grandmother Queen Victoria.

From the eleventh century,
it was traditional at the Feast of
the Epiphany for the sovereign
to make an offering of gold,
frankincense and myrrh, in
commemoration of the gifts given by
the Magi to the infant Jesus. There survives in the
Royal Collection a small tooled box containing frankincense
thought to have been used during the Epiphany service in the
reign of Charles II.

Until the reign of George III, sovereigns conventionally
attended the ceremony in person, with the sword of state carried
before them and a procession of heralds and knights of the Garter,
Thistle and Bath following behind. As The Queen remains at
Sandringham for several weeks after Christmas, the offerings are
today made by two of The Queen's Gentlemen Ushers, who are
escorted to the Chapel Royal at St James's Palace by a detachment

*Box containing
frankincense,*
tooled leather,
late seventeenth
century, RCIN 43870

of The Queen's Yeomen of the Guard. The offerings, known as 'The Queen's Gifts', are presented on two King George IV (1762–1830) silver-gilt patens. The frankincense and myrrh for the offerings are provided by the Apothecary to the Queen. Until 1859, these spices were presented in silk bags, placed in a silk-covered box. A third bag contained a small roll of gold leaf. At Prince Albert's suggestion, the beaten gold was replaced by 25 new gold sovereigns. Several of the sovereigns used today date from the reign of Queen Victoria, while others were minted during the reigns of her successors including Her Majesty The Queen.

For centuries, the Feast of the Epiphany has marked the end of the Christmas festivities and the beginning of a new royal year.

Patens, silver-gilt, 1821, RCIN 92017

Each year at Christmas, Her Majesty The Queen receives a sprig of Holy Thorn from the garden of the church of St John the Baptist in Glastonbury. The tree is known as the Holy Thorn because it blooms twice a year, in both the spring, close to the time of Easter, and in midwinter, around Christmas. An ancient legend connects the thorn with Joseph of Arimathea and the arrival of Christianity in Britain.

The tradition of sending a sprig of the Holy Thorn to the monarch at Christmas is thought to date back to a time before the Reformation. The Abbot of Glastonbury was supposed to have sent the monarch a spray of Christmas flowering thorn for the royal feast table as a show of loyalty and to garner royal favour. After the Reformation, the tradition was revived in the early seventeenth century by James Montague, Bishop of Bath and Wells, who organised an entertainment for Anne of Denmark (1574–1619), Queen Consort of James I and VI (1566–1625), at which the character of Joseph of Arimathea presented the Queen with two sprigs of Holy Thorn. Later in the century, Charles I (1600–1649) is also said to have received a spray of Christmas flowering thorn. However, the practice died out during the days of the Commonwealth, when celebrating Christmas was outlawed and the original Holy Thorn was cut down on the orders of Oliver Cromwell (1599–1658).

Yeomen Of The Guard outside St James's Palace Royal Chapel during King's Epiphany Gifts, 1936

In 1929, the practice was reintroduced when a sprig of Holy
Thorn was sent to Queen Mary (1867–53), wife of King George V.
Since then, a spray of flowering thorn has been sent to a member
of the royal family from the people of Glastonbury each December.
Until 2002, two sprays were delivered, one for The Queen and one
for Queen Elizabeth The Queen Mother (1900–2002).

Cutting of the sprig from the Holy Thorn tree outside the
church of St John the Baptist involves a ceremony attended by the
clergy and representatives from other churches, local dignitaries
including the Mayor of Glastonbury, as well as children from local
schools and their families. A sprig of thorn intended for The Queen
is cut by the eldest child at St John's Infant School, after which 'The
Holy Thorn Song' is sung by the children.

There is a very special tree
We call the Holy Thorn,
That flowers in December
The month that Christ was born.

We're told this very special tree
Grew from a staff of thorn,
Brought by a man called Joseph
From the land where Christ was born.

It now is our tradition
To send a sprig of thorn,
To greet Her Gracious Majesty
On the day that Christ was born.

Sebastian Biddlecombe presenting the annual gift of a Holy Thorn cutting from the people of Glastonbury to The Queen at Buckingham Palace, 15 December 1999

For many years, the sprig of Holy Thorn was sent to The Queen in a shoebox. However, to celebrate the Millennium in 1999, the sprig, with a recording of the 'The Holy Thorn Song' and a Christmas card signed by the children of St John's Infant School, was taken to London and delivered to The Queen in person by that year's thorn cutter.

The Holy Thorn cutting blooms for several weeks and decorates the royal dining table on Christmas Day or else is kept on Her Majesty's desk at Sandringham during the festive season.

CHRISTMAS TREES

PRINCE ALBERT IS OFTEN CREDITED WITH HAVING INTRODUCED THE CHRISTMAS TREE TO BRITAIN FROM GERMANY FOLLOWING HIS MARRIAGE TO QUEEN VICTORIA IN 1840. HOWEVER, CHRISTMAS TREES HAD BEEN PART OF ROYAL FESTIVE CELEBRATIONS SINCE THE LATE EIGHTEENTH CENTURY, WHEN THE FIRST CHRISTMAS TREES WERE SET UP BY QUEEN CHARLOTTE, CONSORT OF GEORGE III.

Like Prince Albert, Queen Charlotte brought the tradition with her from her native Germany, where decorating evergreen trees with candles, paper flowers and sweets had been customary at Christmastime since the early 1600s. In northern Germany, where Queen Charlotte grew up, it was traditional to deck a single yew bough, around which the family would gather on Christmas Eve to exchange gifts.

At this time of year, few sights evoke more feelings of cheer and goodwill than the twinkling lights of a Christmas tree.
— HM QUEEN ELIZABETH II,
25 DECEMBER 2015

Pauline Baynes, *The Christmas Tree in History and Legend*,
Illustrated London News, 14 November 1958

At the Georgian court, Queen Charlotte transformed the traditional yew-bough ritual into a festive spectacle that could be enjoyed not only by family and friends but by the wider court and royal household. On Christmas Eve 1800, Queen Charlotte hosted a festive party at the Queen's Lodge for the children of all the principal families in Windsor. A Christmas tree was the centrepiece of the celebrations. Dr John Watkins, who attended the party, later described the scene:

It is a pleasure to have this blessed festival associated with one's happiest days. The very smell of the Christmas Trees of pleasant memories.
— QUEEN VICTORIA, 24 DECEMBER 1841

'in the middle of the room stood an immense tub with a yew-tree placed in it, from the branches of which hung bunches of sweetmeats, almonds, and raisins, in papers, fruits, and toys, most tastefully arranged, and the whole illuminated by small wax candles. After the company had walked round and admired the tree, each child obtained a portion of the sweets which it bore, together with a toy, and all returned home quite delighted.'

The tradition established by Queen Charlotte was continued by her daughter-in-law Queen Adelaide (1792–1849), consort of William IV (1765–1837). Adelaide, who was also German, hosted yearly Christmas celebrations during her husband's reign. In her memoirs, Wilhelmina Kennedy-Erskine, Countess of Munster, described the parties held at the Royal Pavilion, Brighton, during which a Christmas tree was set up in the Banqueting Room: 'She [Queen Adelaide] used every Christmas Eve to prepare an enormous Christmas tree, which was lit up with tapers, while

New. Decem' 2b. 1847
Princess Mary.

Princess Mary
of Cambridge
decorating a
Christmas tree,
watercolour, 1847,
RCIN 928617

from the boughs were hung gilded fruits – apples, pears, walnuts, &c. – and innumerable gifts of value for her ladies and for the guests young and old.'

Christmas trees were also part of the royal festive celebrations at Kensington Palace during Queen Victoria's childhood. Writing in her journal on Christmas Eve 1832, the 13-year-old Princess Victoria described how two trees hung with lights and sugar ornaments were placed on tables in the Dining Room, around which presents were laid out.

While Prince Albert may not have introduced Christmas trees to Britain, he encouraged the tradition, seeking to replicate for his own children the experiences that he and his brother Ernest II, Duke of Saxe-Coburg and Gotha (1818–93) had shared as boys. Each year from 1840, trees of the German Springelbaum variety were imported from Prince Albert's native Coburg and erected around Windsor Castle, where the royal couple spent Christmas during the years of their marriage. These trees were placed on tables with gifts arranged beneath. Each table and tree were intended for a different recipient, with Queen Victoria, Prince Albert, their children and the Queen's mother, the Duchess of Kent (1786–1861), each having their own. In a letter written to his father on Christmas Eve 1841, Prince Albert described how his two small children, Victoria and Albert Edward (later King Edward VII) known as 'Vicky' and 'Bertie', 'are full of happy wonder at the German Christmas-tree and its radiant candles'.

A Christmas tree was also arranged annually for the royal household, who would assemble in the Oak Room to see it. Writing in 1847 to her mother, the Queen's Maid of Honour Eleanor Stanley described 'a little fir tree, in the German fashion, covered with bonbons, gilt walnuts, and little coloured tapers'. Further Christmas trees were traditionally set up on the sideboard in the Private Dining Room, arranged and decorated by Mr Mawditt, the Queen's Confectioner. A visitor to Windsor Castle in 1860 described how, that year, the rooms 'were lighted up with Christmas trees hung from the ceiling, the chandeliers being taken down'; however, this does not appear to have been an annual tradition.

In addition to those Christmas trees set up at Windsor Castle, Queen Victoria and Prince Albert also gave a number of trees to schools and army barracks. The enthusiasm of the Queen and Prince Consort for Christmas trees did much to popularise the tradition, particularly when in 1848 the *Illustrated London News* printed a picture of the royal family around a Christmas tree. The engraving was accompanied by a detailed description of the tree and its decorations:

'The tree employed for this festive purpose is a young fir, about eight feet high, and has six tiers of branches. On each tier or branch, are arranged a dozen wax tapers. Pendant from the branches are elegant trays, baskets, *bonbonnieres* and other receptacles for sweetmeats, of the most varied and expensive kind; and all forms of colours, and degrees of beauty. Fancy cakes, gilt gingerbread and eggs filled with sweetmeats, are also

Opposite

Queen Victoria and Prince Albert with their children and a Christmas tree at Windsor, Illustrated London News, 1848

suspended by variously-coloured ribbons from the branches. On
the summit of the tree stands a small figure of an angel, with
outstretched wings, holding in each hand a wreath. These trees
are objects of much interest to all visitors to the Castle, from
Christmas Eve, when they are first set up, until Twelfth Night,
when they are finally removed.'

The royal Christmas tree captured the public imagination and the
fashion quickly spread. As early as 1852, odes to the Christmas tree

James Roberts
(*c.*1800–1867),
*Christmas trees of
the Duchess of Kent
and the royal children
at Windsor Castle*,
1850, watercolour
on paper, 1850,
RCIN 919813

Joseph Nash
(1809–78),
Queen Victoria's
Christmas tree,
Windsor Castle,
1845, watercolour
on paper, 1845,
RCIN 919807

appeared in periodicals; in 1854 a huge, glittering tree was set up
in the Crystal Palace and many hundreds of small trees were sold
yearly at Covent Garden. In a letter of 1865, Queen Victoria wrote
that she rejoiced 'to think that the Prince and herself are the cause
of Christmas trees being so generally adopted in this country'.

During their marriage Queen Victoria and Prince Albert
commissioned painted and photographic records of their Christmas
trees at Windsor Castle. The artist James Roberts made several
watercolours of the Christmas trees at the castle, including those set
up for the Duchess of Kent and the royal children in 1850, while
in 1845 Joseph Nash painted Queen Victoria's Christmas tree in
the Blue Closet. In her journal entry for Christmas Eve that year,

Dr Ernst Becker (1826–88), *Queen Victoria's
Christmas tree, Windsor Castle*, albumen paper print
from a dry collodion plate, 1857, RCIN 2906247

Queen Victoria records how 'at 6 Albert took me into the Blue Closet, where as usual my frosted tree stood & my presents were all arranged on a table'. Later, in 1857, Prince Albert's German librarian Dr Ernst Becker, a keen photographer, made a photograph of the Queen's tree, surrounded by gifts from the Prince Consort.

After Prince Albert's death in 1861, Queen Victoria spent almost every Christmas at Osborne House on the Isle of Wight. There she continued the Christmas traditions established during the years of her marriage, including the annual arrangement of Christmas trees for members of her family and household.

Christmas trees in the Indian Room, Durbar Wing, Osborne House, albumen print, 1896–7, RCIN 2802659

In 1899 Queen Victoria spent Christmas at Windsor for the final time. On Boxing Day the Queen hosted a tea in St George's Hall for the families of soldiers serving in the Second Anglo-Boer War. She recorded the event in her journal:

'I went into St. George's Hall to look at the beautiful big Xmas tree, 25 ft. high, hung with all sorts of little presents, sweets, toys & glittering ornaments, which Beatrice [Princess Beatrice (1857–1944)], Helena [Princess Helena (1846–1923)] & the Ladies have worked hard in decorating. […] all the women, & children trooped in, & after looking at the tree they all sat down to tea at 2 very long tables, below the tree. Every one helped to serve them, including my family, old & young & my ladies & gentlemen. I was rolled up & down round the tables after which I went away for a short while to have my own tea, returning when the tree was beginning to be stripped, handing myself many of the things to the wives & dear little children.'

Christmas trees in the Dining Room,
Osborne House, albumen print, *c.*1873,
RCIN 2103818

By the time of Queen Victoria's death in 1901, Christmas trees were not only central to royal festivities but had become an indispensable part of seasonal celebrations across the length and breadth of Britain and beyond. In 1905, King George V and Queen Mary, then Prince and Princess of Wales, spent Christmas in India. During their visit to the city of Gwalior, the Princess hosted a Christmas party at which she presented local children with a tree and presents. In a letter to her son, the future King George VI, she wrote: 'They had never seen a Tree before so you can imagine their delight.'

During the reigns of King Edward VII (1841–1910), George V and George VI (1895–1952), the Christmas season was customarily spent on the Sandringham Estate in Norfolk, acquired as a family home for the future Edward VII and Queen Alexandra (1844–1925) at the time of their marriage in 1863. Her Majesty The Queen has followed in this practice, spending the festive period at Sandringham for most of her reign. Here the traditions established by Queen Victoria and Prince Albert have been continued, although since 1902 only two Christmas trees have been arranged, one for the royal family and one for the household. Today, The Queen, The Duke of Edinburgh (b.1921) and other members of the royal family usually put the finishing touches to their Christmas tree themselves.

Continuing the customs established in the nineteenth century by Queen Victoria and Prince Albert, The Queen presents the schools and churches around Sandringham with Christmas trees. Trees are also given each year to Westminster Abbey and St Paul's Cathedral in London, and to St Giles's Cathedral and the Canongate Kirk in Edinburgh.

Opposite

British Broadcasting Corporation, *HM Queen Elizabeth II and HRH The Duke of Edinburgh decorating the Christmas tree, Windsor Castle*, still from BBC film, 1969, RCIN 2004781

The Season of Gifts

HE ROYAL CHRISTMAS HAS FOR CENTURIES BEEN A TIME OF FEASTING, FESTIVITIES AND THE GIVING AND RECEIVING OF GIFTS. HOWEVER, UNTIL THE NINETEENTH CENTURY, GIFTS WERE NOT EXCHANGED ON CHRISTMAS EVE; RATHER THEY WERE GIVEN ON NEW YEAR'S DAY, IN A TRADITION DATING BACK TO AT LEAST THE THIRTEENTH CENTURY.

In an unusual twist, it was traditional at New Year for the monarch to first be given gifts by their subjects, which they would then reciprocate. This offered courtiers, servants and even ordinary people outside of the court an opportunity to demonstrate their loyalty to the Crown, and for the monarch, as the ultimate source of honour and generosity, to bestow favour or display displeasure. Those expected to give gifts included noblemen, particularly those who had received land from the Crown, and bishops, but many others gave gifts by

The preparation & giving to one's dear ones, of one's little gifts, the Xmas trees & the surprise, of all the beautiful things one receives oneself, — <u>all</u>, is so delightful.

— QUEEN VICTORIA, 24 DECEMBER 1842

Galterus Delaenus (active *c.*1553), *Strena
Galteri Delaeni: ex capite Geneseos quarto
deprompta. 'Ipsis calendis Januarii: anno 1553'*,
manuscript bound in brown calf skin with
gold tooling, 1553, RCIN 1081249

choice, including other members of the royal
family. In 1552, Edward VI received New
Year's Gifts from all the earls and barons, as
well as other senior noblemen; 15 bishops and
five royal chaplains; virtually every member
of his household from high-ranking officials
like the Lord Chamberlain and the Keeper
of the Privy Purse to the Sergeant of the
Pastry and even the royal dog keeper. Gifts
were also presented by the widows of peers,
government officials such as ambassadors and
visiting foreign diplomats. One of the young
King's New Year's gifts from 1553 survives in
the Royal Library at Windsor. The beautifully
bound book, with a design incorporating the
King's coat of arms and cypher, topped with
the Tudor rose and crown, and surrounded
by cornucopias of flowers and fleurs-de-lis, all picked out in gold,
was given to Edward VI by Gualterus Deloenus, who had once been
librarian to Edward's father, Henry VIII.

It was in the reign of Henry VIII that the formal court ceremony
of giving New Year's gifts developed. On the morning of New
Year's Day, gifts were presented to the King by the donor or their
representative in the Presence Chamber in order of precedence, with
the highest-ranking donor offering their gift
first. As the King received each offering, the Treasurer of the
Royal Household would record it on a gift roll, many of which

still survive in the National Archives, London.
The King could choose not to accept gifts
as a sign of displeasure. In 1532 Henry VIII
was offered New Year's gifts by both his
Queen, Catherine of Aragon (1485–1536),
and the woman he hoped to marry,
Anne Boleyn (c.1501–36); in a show of his
feelings, the King rejected the gifts from the
Queen and accepted those from Anne.

Gifts offered to the monarch were
usually gold or silver plate, jewellery
or money, though they might also
receive works of art, fine embroidery or
ornately bound books. In 1539, the artist
Hans Holbein the Younger presented
Henry VIII with a portrait of his baby
son Prince Edward as a New Year's gift.

Top

Hans Holbein the Younger (1497/8–1543),
Edward, Prince of Wales (1537–53), black and
coloured chalks, and pen and ink on pale
pink prepared paper, 1538, RCIN 912200

Right

Hans Holbein the Younger (1497/8–1543),
Edward VI as a Child, oil on panel, c.1538,
National Gallery of Art, Washington

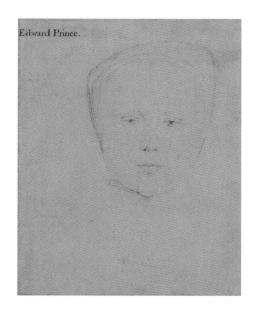

English, *The
Maundy Dish*,
silver-gilt, 1660,
RCIN 31747

The preparatory drawing survives in the Royal Collection, while the painting itself is now in the National Gallery of Art in Washington. In the Royal Collection there is an alms dish, delivered to Philip Waters, Gentleman Porter to Charles II, on 31 December 1685, which was used during the annual New Year's Gift ceremony until the end of the seventeenth century.

On the afternoon of New Year's Day, those who had given gifts to the monarch would attend the Jewel House at the Tower of London to receive their gift in return. This was usually money and an item of plate, supplied by the goldsmiths of the Jewel House. Plate was given by weight, with the most favoured courtiers receiving the greatest weight. In 1585, Elizabeth I gave her favourites Sir Christopher Hatton and the Earl of Leicester as much as 400 ounces of plate; no other peer received more than 50 ounces. By the reign of James I, the system for giving and receiving gifts had become highly regulated. An earl, for example, might be expected to purchase a new purse for around five shillings and then fill it with coins to the value of 20 pounds (around £2,750 today). In return, he was entitled to 18 shillings and 6 pence, and a piece of gold or silver plate weighing 30 ounces. At New Year 1661, the first since the restoration of the monarchy, diarist Samuel Pepys delivered the King's gift on behalf of his patron, the Earl of Sandwich.

As he recorded in his diary on 4 January, he had gone early in the
morning to

> 'the Jewell Office, to choose a piece of gilt plate for my Lord, in
> return of his offering to the King (which it seems is usual at this
> time of year, and an Earl gives twenty pieces in gold in a purse
> to the King). I chose a gilt tankard, weighing 31 ounces and a
> half, and he is allowed 30; so I paid 12s. for the ounce and
> half over what he is to have'

A two-handled silver-gilt cup weighing 46 ounces
given by Charles II to Richard Sterne, Archbishop of
York, as a New Year's gift in around 1674 survives in
the Victoria and Albert Museum, London.

The ancient tradition of the sovereign giving plate
to those bringing New Year's gifts was abolished in 1685;
however, the annual New Year's gift ceremony continued until
1700.

Though by the nineteenth century it was no longer customary
for the sovereign to receive New Year's gifts, throughout her reign
Queen Victoria annually distributed gifts at New Year to the poor.
Such gifts usually took the form of meat, bread, coal and blankets.
In Windsor, the distribution took place in the riding school, which
the Queen and members of the royal family attended yearly until
1861. In 1846, the artist Joseph Nash joined the royal party and
later produced a watercolour of the occasion. Writing in her diary
on 1 January 1844, Queen Victoria described the scene:

English, *The Sterne
Cup*, silver-gilt, 1673–4,
Victoria and Albert
Museum, London

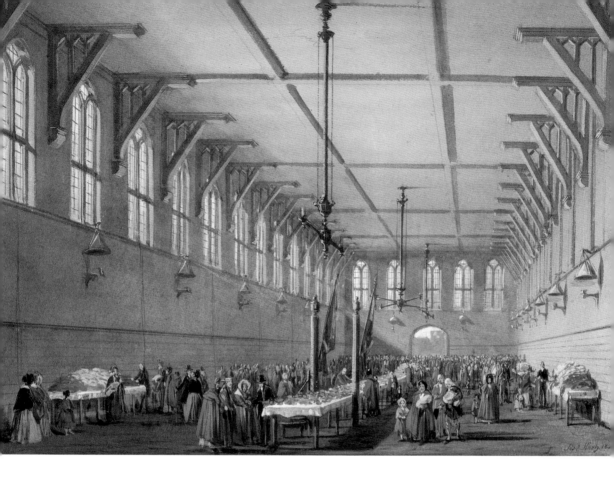

Joseph Nash (1809–78),
*The distribution of bounty
at the Riding School,
Windsor, 1 January
1846,* watercolour and
bodycolour on paper,
1846, RCIN 919771

'We walked in sun, which had succeeded rain, down to the
Riding School, & went up to the room, where were spread upon
tables, the meat, bread, plum pudding & blankets which were to
be distributed to the poor people. There were 180 families, who
received blankets, & 186, provisions, including Children, which
in all, came to near upon 1000 persons. It was a pretty sight
watching the distribution & the way in which it was carried out,
having just the right effect upon the poor people. Hitherto it had
been so badly done that they hardly knew the gifts came from us.'

The arrival from Germany of the Christmas tree at the British royal court brought with it the start of another festive tradition, *Heiligabend Bescherung* – the giving of presents on Holy Evening or Christmas Eve. When Christmas trees were introduced to the Georgian court by Queen Charlotte at the beginning of the nineteenth century, it became usual to give presents on Christmas Eve, when the trees were lit for the first time.

In her description of the parties given on Christmas Eve by William IV and Queen Adelaide during the 1830s, Wilhelmina Kennedy-Erskine, Countess of Munster, wrote:

> 'I think the happiest moment of those most happy evenings was when, after a kind embrace from the King and Queen, each pair of children was set free to search for, and find his or her own table. Small round tables, upholstered in white, were dotted about all over the room with each child's name pinned upon the one dedicated to him or her, and covered with bon-bons and toys of every variety; no one can conceive the delight and shouting when each child discovered its own property.'

By this time, the custom of giving gifts on Christmas Eve had been established as an important part of the festive celebrations of the royal family. Yearly on 24 December beginning in 1832, Queen Victoria recorded in her journal the presents she both gave and received. On Christmas Eve 1836, the year before she became Queen, the 17-year-old Princess Victoria described in detail the presents received from her mother, the Duchess of Kent:

Friendship's Offering,
and Winter's Wreath,
London, Smith,
Elder & Co.,
1836, a Christmas
and New Year's
present for 1836,
RCIN 1056299

'Very soon after dinner Mamma sent for us into the Gallery, where all the things were arranged on different tables. From my dear Mamma I received a beautiful massive gold buckle in the shape of two serpents; a lovely delicate little gold chain with a turquoise clasp; a fine album of brown moroccow with a silver clasp; a lovely coloured sketch of dearest Aunt Louise by Partridge [...] 3 beautiful drawings by Munn, one lovely sea view by Purser, and one beautiful cattle piece by Cooper [...] 3 prints; a book called 'Finden's Tableaux'; 'Heath's picturesq Annual for Ireland'; both these are very pretty; 'Friendship's Offering' and 'The English Annual for 1837'; 'The Holy Land', illustrated beautifully; two handkerchiefs, a very pretty black satin apron trimmed with red velvet; and two almanacks. I am very thankful to my dear Mamma for all these very pretty things.'

With Queen Victoria's marriage to Prince Albert and the birth
of their nine children, the Christmas Eve *Bescherung* became an
even more central part of the royal Christmas. In her journal entry
for 24 December 1843, the Queen described the 'excitement &
agitation of finishing arraying the "Bescherung" & presents, which
to me is such a pleasure'. At Windsor Castle, where the royal court
spent Christmas until Prince Albert's death in 1861, gift tables for
each member of the family were arranged with Christmas trees across
several rooms. Those for the Queen's mother, the Duchess of Kent,
and for the royal children were usually grouped together in one room,
while the Queen and the Prince Consort set up present tables for
each other in separate rooms. Queen Victoria's *Bescherung*, arranged
by Prince Albert on Christmas Eve 1850, which she described as
'really too much, too magnificent', is recorded in a painting by William
Corden. In it many of the gifts received by the Queen can be clearly
seen, including a watercolour by Edward Henry Corbould of a scene
from Giacomo Meyerbeer's opera *Le Prophète*. Meyerbeer was one
of Victoria's favourite composers and she had seen his newest opera
several times over the summer of 1850. The scene depicted in the
watercolour had captured the Queen's imagination; in a letter to her
uncle, Leopold I, King of the Belgians (1790–1865), she described it as
'highly dramatic & really very moving' and was consequently delighted
when she received the watercolour from Albert that Christmas.

The Christmas gifts exchanged by Queen Victoria and
Prince Albert often conveyed such personal sentiments. In the
course of their marriage, they gave each other jewellery, *objets d'art*
and portraits of their immediate and extended family commissioned

from some of the leading artists of the day, as well as works of art intended to appeal to the other's personal tastes. Sometimes gifts were surprises, but more often they were chosen in advance.

The first Christmas present that Victoria received from Albert was sent by him from his native Coburg shortly after their engagement. In a letter written to his fiancée on 10 December 1839, Albert wrote, 'I venture, now that Christmas is at the door, to enclose a small bracelet for you, begging you to think not of the object, but of the feelings of love and attachment it dedicates to you.' The delicate gold bracelet, set with an emerald and three

Edward Henry Corbould (1815–1905), *The coronation scene from Meyerbeer's 'Le Prophète'*, watercolour on paper, 1850, RCIN 451109

William Corden
the Younger
(1819–1900),
*Queen Victoria's
Christmas tree*, oil
on panel, 1851,
RCIN 402566

Joachim Friedrich Kerstein (1805–60),
The Atholl Inkstand, silver, silver-gilt, granite,
marble, quartz, deer teeth, cairngorm and
amethystine quartz, 1844–5, RCIN 15955

William Essex
(1784–1869),
*Brooch of Victoria,
Princess Royal*,
enamel, gold,
sapphires, rubies,
emeralds, diamonds
and topazes, 1842,
RCIN 4834

diamonds, is engraved with hearts and lovers'
knots and is inscribed on the reverse 'From
Albert / Decr 24 1839'.

Much of the jewellery given to the Queen
by the Prince Consort was made to his own designs and
celebrated their growing family or commemorated trips the
couple had taken together. Of the presents Queen Victoria received
from Prince Albert for Christmas 1841, the one that she valued
most was a bejewelled brooch with an enamel portrait miniature of
their first child, Victoria, Princess Royal, in the guise of a cherub. In
her journal the Queen declared that 'the workmanship & design are
quite exquisite, & dear Albert was so pleased at my delight over it, it
having been entirely his own idea & taste'.

Four years later, for Christmas 1845, Prince Albert designed for
the Queen an elaborately decorated inkstand, known as the Atholl
Inkstand. The gift was intended as a reminder of the happy time the
royal couple had spent at Blair Castle in the Scottish Highlands in
September 1844, which Victoria described as 'a little Arcadia for
a few weeks'. The inkstand consists of a large, frosted silver stag,
which stands on stones collected by Albert during the couple's stay.
The marble plaques around the base of the stand were based on
watercolours made during the trip by the painter Charles Landseer,

French, *Bracelet*,
gold, emeralds and
diamonds, 1839,
RCIN 65300

who accompanied the royal party. The piece is prominently displayed in the watercolour by Joseph Nash of Queen Victoria's Christmas tree and present tables set up that year in the Blue Closet at Windsor Castle (see p. 25).

For their first Christmas together, Queen Victoria presented Prince Albert with her portrait, painted by the artist John Partridge. In it she wears several items of jewellery given to her by the Prince during the first year of their marriage, including a bracelet set with his portrait and a glass locket containing a lock of his hair, which Victoria wore day and night during their engagement. A year later, in 1842, the Queen surprised her husband with a picture of his favourite greyhound, Eos, by the noted animal painter Sir Edwin Landseer. The painting shows Eos standing poised and alert, guarding her master's possessions – a pair of leather gloves, a top hat and an ivory-topped cane. Landseer is said to have borrowed these items

Sir Edwin Landseer (1803–73), *Eos,* oil on canvas, 1841, RCIN 403219

John Partridge
(1790–1872),
Queen Victoria
(1819–1901), oil
on canvas, 1840,
RCIN 403022

without the Prince's knowledge, causing panic amongst his personal servants when they could not be found. The secrecy paid off; however, writing in her journal on Christmas Eve, Queen Victoria described Prince Albert's delight and surprise on receiving the painting.

Until the nineteenth century, festive celebrations had been primarily adult occasions, centred on feasting and games, but, with the arrival of the Christmas tree and the *Heiligabend Bescherung*, Christmas became a family festival, increasingly focused on children. Prince Albert in particular, who remembered fondly his childhood

Christmases with his brother in Coburg, sought in his children 'an echo of what Ernest and I were in the old time, of what we felt and thought' and strove to recreate such happy, family Christmases for the young Princes and Princesses. On Christmas Eve 1856, for the amusement of his children, Prince Albert arranged for one of his gamekeepers on the Windsor estate to dress up as St Nicholas, in accordance with traditional Germany folktales. Writing in her journal, Queen Victoria described the occasion:

> 'In Germany the old saying that St. Nicholas appears with a rod
> for naughty children, & gingerbread for good ones, is constantly
> represented, & Arthur hearing of this begged for one. Accordingly
> Albert got up a St. Nicholas, most formidable he looking, in black,
> covered with snow, a long white beard, & red nose, — of a gigantic
> stature! He came in asking the Children, who were somewhat awed
> & alarmed, — 'are you a good child', & giving them gingerbread &
> apples. I since heard that it was Cowley (the Jäger) who Albert had
> taught his part beautifully, but the children went on guessing every
> kind of person, & even now have not been told for certain.'

Bountiful Christmas presents were enjoyed by the royal children. In her journals, Queen Victoria described afternoons spent choosing

Above

Ferdinand II, King Consort of Portugal (1816–85), *St Nicholas distributing gifts*, etching, 1848, RCIN 809356.az

Opposite

Albert Edward, Prince of Wales (1841–1910), *Study of a blinded soldier*, pencil and watercolour on paper, 1853, RCIN 981047

After Roger
Fenton (1819–69),
*Prince Arthur in
the undress uniform
of the Grenadier
Guards*, carbon
print of an original
albumen print, 1868,
RCIN 2800659

presents for her family and wrote with pleasure of
her children's joy on Christmas Eve when they were
taken to their Christmas tree. In 1853 she wrote:

> 'we went with Mama in the room where the
> Children's tree was, the 7 Children jumping &
> shouting with delight. Toys, without end, for the
> little ones, books, prints, articles for work, games
> for Boys &c. were given to them all & an undress
> uniform of the Grenadier Guards, to little Arthur.'

The royal children also gave presents to their
parents, their grandmother, the Duchess of Kent,
and their personal servants, including their governess
Madame Maria de Hocédé. These were almost
invariably things they had made themselves, including
drawings, paintings and items of needlework like
handkerchiefs and slippers embroidered by the
Princesses. All of the royal children were encouraged
to draw and paint by Queen Victoria and
Prince Albert, both talented amateur artists, and
they received lessons from a drawing master. During
the annual Christmas Eve *Bescherung,* the Princes
and Princesses would present their parents with
drawings and watercolours. These often included
messages for the recipient, like the drawing of
a wounded soldier given by the 12-year-old

49

Prince of Wales to Prince Albert, which is inscribed 'For dear Papa, from Bertie. Christmas Eve 1853'. As the royal children grew up and became more proficient, the artwork for their parents became more elaborate. A painting made by Princess Alice (1843–78) for Christmas 1860, when she was 17, depicts a scene from a German folktale, popular in her father's native Coburg. Queen Victoria preserved many of the drawings and paintings presented to herself and Prince Albert by their nine children, having them bound into a series of albums which survive in the Print Room at Windsor Castle.

As well as giving gifts to each other, the royal family also gave Christmas presents to their extended family and personal staff, details of which were meticulously kept in yearly ledgers. In a letter to her mother, Eleanor Stanley, Queen Victoria's Maid of Honor, described the gifts she received from the Queen and Prince Consort for Christmas 1847:

'Round [the tree] were all our presents, with the name of each person, written by the Queen on a slip of paper lying by the present; Caroline's and mine were two very pretty little chains for round the neck, with a hand in front, which holds the ring, to which is fastened a heart or locket; mine is in carbuncles and little diamonds. [...] We also got, in common with all the others, a

Ledger of gifts given by Queen Victoria, c.1841–2, Royal Archives, RA VIC/ADDT/312

Princess Alice (1843–78), *Die 4 Burg-Fräulein*, pencil, watercolour and bodycolour on paper, 1860, RCIN 980952

new print of the Prince of Wales and Prince Alfred in Highland costume, from a sketch by Sir William Ross, and one of the Queen, from a watercolour drawing by Winterhalter; both very pretty. […] We each also got an almanac and some gingerbread. After that we followed the Queen and Prince to see their own presents, and the children's and the Duchess of Kent's.'

This tradition continues today, with Her Majesty The Queen giving Christmas presents to all members of the Royal Household, personally handing out gifts to long-serving members staff.

As her children married and had children of their own, Queen Victoria delighted in sharing with her growing family the Christmas traditions established by herself and Prince Albert, including the annual *Heiligabend Bescherung*.

Sir William Ross (1794–1860), *Albert Edward, Prince of Wales, and Prince Alfred*, watercolour, 1847, RCIN 913818

51

After the Prince Consort's death in 1861, Victoria traditionally spent Christmas at Osborne House, where members of the royal family gathered for the celebrations. Here, the Christmas tree and present tables were set up in the Dining Room until 1890, when the festivities moved to the newly added Durbar Room.

Since each of Queen Victoria's nine children married into different European royal houses, and many of her 42 grandchildren in turn did the same, by the close of the nineteenth century the Queen's family were scattered across the length and breadth of Europe. Each year at Christmas, Queen Victoria sent presents to her sons and daughters and their spouses, her grandchildren and great-grandchildren, wherever they might be. In 1881, the Wales

The Dining Room, Osborne House, with Christmas presents and tree, albumen print, 1878, RCIN 2103819

family spent Christmas at their Sandringham Estate in Norfolk, rather than joining the Queen at Osborne. Amongst the gifts sent by Victoria to Sandringham was an ornate festive fan, decorated with holly, mistletoe and Christmas roses, for her daughter-in-law the Princess of Wales, later Queen Alexandra.

In the Royal Archives at Windsor are bound volumes of correspondence to Queen Victoria from her grandchildren, including numerous letters from both home and abroad thanking the Queen for gifts received at Christmas. On 30 December 1877, Princess Irene of Hesse and by Rhine (1866–1953) wrote from the Neues Palais, Darmstadt, Germany to thank her grandmother for 'your beautiful presents', which that year included pocket handkerchiefs and a volume of short stories. A year later, the future King George V wrote to his grandmother from Sandringham to thank her for 'the very pretty writing case and the stories from Shakespeare which I like very much'.

Alice Loch (1840–1932), Christmas fan, pale green satin leaf, plain mother-of-pearl guards and sticks, silver pin with mother-of-pearl head, 1881, RCIN 25197

Letter from Princess Irene of Hesse and by Rhine to Queen Victoria, 30 December 1877, Royal Archives, RA VIC/MAIN/Z/79/99

Franz Xaver
Winterhalter (1805–73),
*Princess Charlotte of
Belgium* (1840–1927),
oil on canvas, 1842,
RCIN 403603

Queen Victoria also received gifts from her extended family overseas. For Christmas 1842, Louise, Queen of the Belgians (1812–50), Victoria's aunt by marriage, sent the Queen a portrait of her two-year-old daughter Princess Charlotte (1840–1927) by a favourite artist, Franz Xaver Winterhalter. In the accompanying letter, Queen Louise wrote that 'your great kindness for us and Charlotte and your amiable wish so often expressed to have her picture by Winterhalter lithographed led me to believe, the picture itself might be agreable to you'. Many years later, in 1896, Queen Victoria's granddaughter Alexandra Feodorovna, Tsarina of Russia (1872–1918), and her husband Tsar Nicholas II (1868–1918) sent the Queen a notebook, enclosed in an ornate silver-gilt and enamel case by the Russian Imperial goldsmith Fabergé. Earlier that year, 'dear Alicky & Nicky' had visited Queen Victoria at Balmoral in Scotland, and during their stay Victoria had admired her granddaughter's jewels, many of which were supplied by Fabergé. The following year, in June 1897, Queen Victoria celebrated her Diamond Jubilee, and guests attending the celebrations were invited to sign the notebook.

In the early twentieth century the royal family continued the practice of Queen Victoria and Prince Albert in giving each other works of art which have subsequently become part of

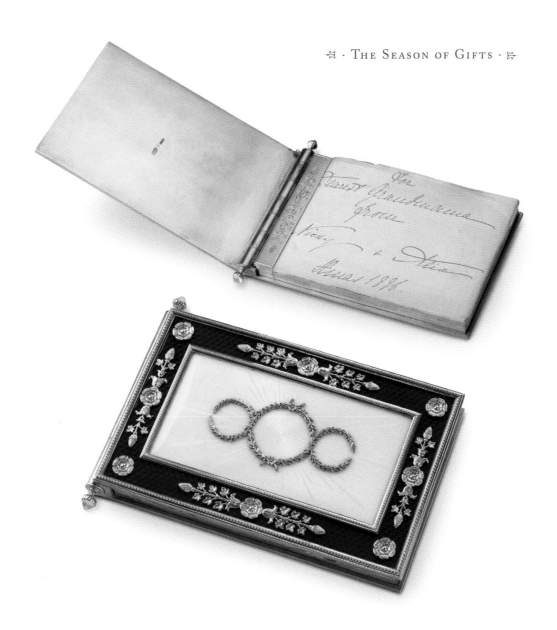

Johann Victor Aarne (1863–1934) for Fabergé, *Notebook*, silver-
gilt with deep red weave and oyster sunburst guilloché enamel,
foliate and ribbon silver-gilt mounts, pencil with moonstone
finials at ends inserted into hinge, 1876–96, RCIN 4819

Bourne & Shepherd (active 1864–1900s), *View from the terrace of the Hussainabad Imambara, Lucknow*, albumen print, 1875–6, RCIN 2114123

Bourne & Shepherd (active 1864–1900s), *Bourne and Shepherd's Royal Photographic Album of Scenes and Personages connected with H.R.H. the Prince of Wales' Tour in India (1841–1910)*, red leather album containing albumen prints, 1875–6, RCIN 2114099

the Royal Collection. For Christmas 1876, Edward VII, then Prince of Wales gave his wife Princess Alexandra an album of photographs taken on his recent year-long trip to India. The Princess was a keen amateur photographer, so the album was a fitting gift, particularly as she had not accompanied her husband on his visit.

Objets d'art, including many pieces by Fabergé, were frequently exchanged by the royal family at Christmas. On Christmas Eve

Right

Fabergé, *Elephant automaton*,
silver, gold, guilloché
enamel, rose diamonds,
cabochon rubies, ivory,
1905, RCIN 40486

Below right

Mikhail Evlampievich
Perkhin (1860–1903) for
Fabergé, *Easter egg*, gold,
guilloché enamel, diamonds,
1899, RCIN 9032

1929, King George V was presented with a Fabergé
elephant automaton by his wife and children. Made
from silver and gold and decorated with enamel,
rose diamonds and rubies, when the clockwork
mechanism is wound the elephant walks, swinging
its head and trunk. Not to be outdone, for Christmas
1933 King George V gave Queen Mary a gold and
guilloché enamel Easter egg, studded with diamonds,
designed by Mikhail Perkhin, the head workmaster
 at Fabergé in the late nineteenth century. Six years
later, on Christmas Eve 1939, Queen Elizabeth,
The Queen Mother was given an exquisite Fabergé fan,

decorated with mother-of-pearl, pink and white enamel and diamonds. A collective gift from her family, two days later the Queen wrote to her mother-in-law Queen Mary to thank her for her part in 'such a delightful present'.

Relatively few paintings were commissioned by the royal family as Christmas presents after the nineteenth century, but in 1914 King George V received a portrait of Queen Mary by the artist Sir William Llewellyn. The painting was a joint Christmas present from his wife and their eldest son the Prince of Wales, later Edward VIII.

Since the accession of King Edward VII in 1901, the royal family has traditionally spent Christmas at Sandringham in Norfolk, where the Christmas Eve *Bescherung* has continued much as it was in the reign of Queen Victoria. Writing in 1901, the future George V described the scene in the Hall, where the tree and present tables were set up, as 'quite like a shop, with all the tables covered with beautiful things'. A visitor to Sandringham recalled the scene 25 years later, when King George V and Queen Mary led the assembled company in a crocodile to the Ball Room, which was lined on three sides with tables, covered in white tablecloths, with red ribbons separating the gifts for each person.

Today, the Royal Family still upholds the traditions of *Heiligabend Bescherung* popularised by Queen Victoria and Prince Albert, assembling on Christmas Eve to lay out their presents – usually token gifts – on trestle tables before they are exchanged at teatime.

Above

Mikhail Evlampievich Perkhin (1860–1903) for Fabergé, *Fan*, cream silk and silk gauze leaf; front guard mother-of-pearl and two-colour gold enamelled in pink and white over a guilloché ground decorated with diamonds, 1895–1905, RCIN 25298

Opposite

Sir William Llewellyn (1858–1941), *Queen Mary* (1867–1953), oil on canvas, 1914, RCIN 404471

The first Christmas card was sent in 1843 by the prominent civil servant, educator and inventor Henry Cole. Cole, who was also a close friend and supporter of Prince Albert, had been instrumental in reforming the British postal system and establishing the Uniform Penny Post in 1840. The new service had encouraged the sending of seasonal greetings at Christmas time, and, with unanswered post piling up in the busy weeks before Christmas, the ever-inventive Cole realised that a festive time-saving solution was needed. Inspired by the decorative letterhead on which much of his seasonal correspondence was written, he turned to his friend, the artist John Callcott Horsley, to help him develop his idea. Horsley produced a design for the first Christmas card, depicting three generations of the Cole family raising a toast, on either side of which were scenes showing acts of charity in keeping with the spirit of the season. Pleased with the result, Cole commissioned a printer to transfer the design onto cards, printing a thousand copies that could be personalised with a hand-written greeting.

Cole's Christmas card was published and offered for sale at a shilling apiece, which was expensive at the time, and the venture was a commercial failure, at least initially. However, the royal family's love of Christmas meant that they were quick to adopt this new, seasonal greeting card. Many of the earliest Christmas cards surviving in the Royal Collection were

Christmas card from Princess Louise to the Duchess of Kent, pen and ink with printed border, 1854, RCIN 814443

Above left

New Year's card from Victoria, Princess Royal, pencil and watercolour on paper, 1855, RCIN 981306.ak

Above right

New Year's card from Victoria, Princess Royal, pencil and watercolour on paper, 1858, RCIN 981248

made by Queen Victoria's children to be given to their parents, extended family and personal staff. The more established tradition of sending seasonal good wishes at New Year was also popular within Queen Victoria's family, and New Year cards were made yearly by the young Princes and Princesses. The handmade Christmas and New Year cards made by the royal children in the 1850s and 1860s were similar to the earliest commercially produced cards, featuring 'paper lace' (embossed and pierced paper) and religious symbols

Opposite

New Year's card from Princess Alice, pencil and watercolour on paper, 1860, RCIN 980931

like angels. A New Year card made by Princess Alice and given to Queen Victoria and Prince Albert on New Year's Day 1860 depicts an angel carrying a flaming torch representing the New Year. A cloud of smoke issuing from the torch spells the numbers 1860, while the torch for 1859 has been discarded and lies smouldering.

By the 1870s, Christmas cards had become an established part of the festive season, and Victorians exchanged, displayed and collected Christmas cards in vast numbers. Queen Victoria was no exception, sending cards not only to her family and friends but also to her household. In her journal for 23 December 1881, Victoria wrote that she was overwhelmed by the number of cards she had to send, and two days later she noted that she had received many cards from her children, relations and friends. In 1898, the Queen's eldest daughter, the Dowager Empress of Germany, known as Vicky, sent her mother a Christmas card from Germany featuring a photograph of herself, with a hand-painted landscape scene and a border of holly and mistletoe.

Theodore Heinrich Voigt (1839–88), *Victoria, Dowager Empress of Germany, with a border of holly and mistletoe*, albumen print mounted onto card, 1898, RCIN 2374649

63

York Cottage.
Sandringham.
Norfolk.

For Dearest Mama & Aunt "Maria" from May & George with loving good wishes for Xmas 1895.

Below

Marcus Adams (1875–1959),
*Portrait photograph of Princess
Elizabeth and Princess Margaret as
a Christmas card*, gelatin silver print
on card, 1939, RCIN 2108383

Above and **right**

*Christmas card with view of
Sandringham from George V
and Queen Mary to Queen
Alexandra*, photographic
print, 1895, RCIN 2104051

With best wishes for Christmas from Princess Elizabeth and Princess Margaret Rose

Queen Alexandra and Queen Mary
were both enthusiastic devotees of the
Christmas card. In 1947, Queen Mary
donated her extensive collection of
Christmas cards to the British Museum.

King George VI and Queen Elizabeth
The Queen Mother, when still Duke and
Duchess of York, began sending Christmas
cards featuring their favourite family
photograph of the year, often taken by royal
photographer Marcus Adams. Her Majesty
The Queen and other members of the
Royal Family continue this tradition.

Each year, the Queen and the Duke of Edinburgh send approximately 750 Christmas cards featuring a family photograph taken in the course of the year. The card is signed 'Elizabeth R' and 'Philip' and features their official cyphers. The official recipients of the royal Christmas card may include British and Commonwealth prime ministers, governors-general and high commissioners, as well as family, friends and members of the Royal Household. The Duke of Edinburgh sends a further 200 cards at Christmas to different regiments and organisations close to him.

Marcus Adams (1875–1959), *Princess Elizabeth's Christmas card with photograph of Princess Elizabeth and Prince Charles*, gelatin silver print on card, 1949, RCIN 2943751

FESTIVE FEASTING

EASTING AT CHRISTMAS HAS BEEN AN IMPORTANT PART OF ROYAL FESTIVE CELEBRATIONS FOR CENTURIES. THE HOUSEHOLD ACCOUNTS OF MANY MEDIEVAL KINGS SHOW LAVISH SPENDING ON PROVISIONS FOR THE FESTIVE FEAST.

When Henry III celebrated Christmas at Woodstock Palace in 1264, the Sheriff of Oxford supplied 30 oxen, 100 sheep, five boars and nine dozen fowls; salted venison came from Wiltshire, salmon and lampreys from Gloucester, six tuns (or large wine casks) of new wine from Bristol and 13 from Northampton. On another occasion, the Sheriff of Sussex was instructed to buy ten peacocks for a Christmas feast at Westminster. These were roasted, gilded and served in their own plumage. Other popular foods at royal Christmas feasts included brawn – a kind of terrine made from the meat of a pig's head, served with mustard; roast goose, capon, bustard or swan; roast sirloin of beef and frumenty. The latter, which could be served either as a savoury

It was a regular Christmas dinner, with turkeys, Baron of Beef, Plum Pudding & Mince Pies.
— QUEEN VICTORIA,
25 DECEMBER 1843

After Joseph Nash (1809–78), *The Private Dining Room at Windsor Castle*, colour lithograph, 1848, RCIN 817132

accompaniment to meat or as a sweet dish, was made from cracked wheat boiled either with broth or with milk, to which could be added eggs, sugar, dried fruit, spices and spirits. It was popularly served throughout the festive period, becoming particularly associated with Twelfth Night celebrations, and remained on the royal feast table until the late eighteenth century.

In a tradition dating back to the Middle Ages, the people of Gloucester presented the sovereign with a large lamprey pie each year at Christmastime. Lampreys, an eel-like fish, were a medieval

67

royal delicacy; Henry I (1068–1135) was said to have died as
a result of eating a surfeit of them. Lampreys were plentiful in
English rivers until the nineteenth century, but those found in
the River Severn were especially prized, and Gloucester became
particularly associated with the dish. This led the Corporation of the
City of Gloucester to send a lamprey pie to the monarch on special
occasions including Christmas. In 1200, King John (1166–1216)
fined the city 40 marks, the equivalent of around £250,000, for
failing to deliver his Christmas lamprey pie. Though the custom
largely died out in the nineteenth century, traditional lamprey pies
are still prepared to mark royal occasions, including the Queen's
Coronation in 1953 and the Golden and Diamond Jubilees.

In the twelfth century, the boar's head became the star of the
royal Christmas feast after it was introduced by Henry II (1133–
1189). Pickled in brine, stuffed, braised and finally roasted, the
boar's head was traditionally presented festooned with herbs; with
carved vegetables for eyes and the mouth stuffed with an apple. Its
arrival at the banqueting table was heralded by trumpets and, from
the sixteenth century, by the singing of the Boar's Head Carol.

The boar's head in hand I bring,
Bedeck'd with bays and rosemary
And I pray you, my masters, merry be
Quot estis in convivio (As many as are in the feast)

The boar's head remains on the royal Christmas Day menu today;
having been relegated to the sideboard in the nineteenth century,

Menu card for New Year's Day, Osborne, 1898, Royal Archives, RA F&V/PRFF/MAIN/1898.0101/MENU

Menu for Queen Victoria's dinner, Christmas Day, 1899, 1919 (after an original of 1899), Royal Archives, RA F&V/PRFF/MAIN/1899.1225/MENU

it is served cold. This ancient royal dish held a fascination for the public. In the later years of her reign, the boar's head for Queen Victoria's Christmas banquet was supplied by her grandson Kaiser Wilhelm II and, in 1896, a newspaper as far afield as Salt Lake City, Utah, reported that 'the Queen has received her usual Christmas present of a boar's head from her grandson, the Emperor of Germany'. Queen Victoria received other gifts for the royal Christmas table from relatives across Europe, including imperial sturgeons from the Tsar of Russia; pâté de foie gras from the Grand Duke of Mecklenburg-Schwerin; and a dozen bottles of Tokay wine from the Emperor of Austria's personal vineyards.

During the years of Queen Victoria's reign, the ancient boar's head was accompanied on the sideboard by a huge baron of beef – a joint consisting of two sirloins joined at the backbone, from an ox reared on the Windsor Estate. From 1841, Prince Albert entered oxen at the Smithfield Cattle Club Show, held annually in early December, and it was traditional for one of his frequently prize-winning animals to grace the royal Christmas table. In 1855, the *Liverpool Mercury* reported that 'this old English joint was this year supplied to Windsor Castle by the royal purveyors at Windsor. The baron was cut from a five-year-old Highland Scot, fed by his Royal Highness Prince Albert, at the Norfolk Farm, and weighed 425lb.'

Roasting the baron of beef, Windsor Castle, 1887,
Illustrated Sporting and Dramatic News, 3 December 1887

In 1852, joints from a Devon ox exhibited by the Prince that year at the Smithfield Cattle Club Show were sent as Christmas presents to the Kings of Prussia and Belgium, with another joint reserved for Queen Victoria's festive feast. The process of roasting the baron might take as long as 15 hours in front of an open range, and a visit to the kitchen at Windsor to see the beef roasting was almost an obligatory part of the festive season. In 1851, Queen Victoria's second son Prince Alfred (1844–1900), affectionately known to his family as Affie, made such a visit with his tutor:

> 'I saw the baron of beef and boar's head, and I went down to
> the larder where I saw hares, pheasants, grouse and a great
> quantity of fat meat; and we saw the pastry room and a model of
> Windsor Castle in sugar.'

The baron of beef was served as a cold cut, decorated with holly and ivy. Following the death of Prince Albert, it was customary for the royal family to spend Christmas at Osborne House on the Isle of Wight. However, as the kitchens there were too small to cook the baron of beef and other Christmas fare, dishes were prepared at Windsor Castle and then sent down to the south coast by train before finally being ferried across the Solent on the Royal Yacht, leading younger members of the royal family to nickname the vessel the 'milk cart'.

Alongside the boar's head and the baron of beef on Queen Victoria's festive sideboard was usually an enormous woodcock pie, containing one hundred birds. In a tradition which continued into the 1930s, the pie was sent each year to the sovereign at Christmas by the

Gustav William
Henry Mullins
(1854–1921),
*The Christmas
sideboard at Osborne*,
photographic print,
1888, Historic England

Lord Lieutenant of Ireland. It was customary for the pie, together
with the boar's head and the baron of beef, to be placed on the
sideboard in the Dining Room at each dinner during the whole
week of Christmas. In 1888 Queen Victoria's Christmas sideboard
was photographed, complete with a boar's head, woodcock pie and
baron of beef, and with the year marked out in flowers.

73

Game pies were another age-old dish on the royal Christmas menu. The records of the Salters' Company contain a recipe for game pie made for Christmas during the reign of Richard II. In the early twentieth century, extravagant raised pies were made for the royal Christmas table using game birds shot on the Sandringham Estate. Gabriel Tschumi, who was Chef to Queen Victoria, King Edward VII and King George V, described the many steps involved in making them:

'The birds used in them – turkey, chicken, pheasant and woodcock – have each to be boned and a stuffing of forcemeat, truffles and tongue […] The woodcock was put inside the pheasant, the pheasant inside the chicken, and the chicken inside the turkey, packed around with stuffing. A very rich pastry was used, and when the pie was sliced, each piece had the different flavours of the bird from which it was made.'

Until 1861, Queen Victoria and Prince Albert spent the Christmas season at Windsor Castle. Here, festive feasts including the Christmas and New Year's Day banquets were served in the Private Dining Room. The Queen's table was always magnificently laid with silver-gilt plate from the Grand Service, commissioned by George IV from royal goldsmiths

Prince Albert (1819–61) (designer), R & S Garrard & Co. (maker), *Table centrepiece*, silver-gilt, 1842–3, RCIN 1570

Samuel Boyce
Landeck and William
Comyns (active
1880s–90s), *Pair
of sleigh sauce boats*,
silver-gilt, 1895–6,
RCINS 48849.1,
48849.2

Rundell, Bridge & Rundell. As well as the dining plate itself, the
display would include decorative items including dessert stands
and centrepieces. In 1842, Prince Albert designed a centrepiece
including little sculptures of four of the royal couple's favourite
pets: Eos, the Prince's devoted greyhound, a dachshund named
Waldman, and two Highland terriers, Cairnach and Islay. Later, two
silver and parcel-gilt sauce boats in the form of sleighs, acquired by
Queen Mary, were added to the royal Christmas table.

Some courses, including dessert, were traditionally served
on porcelain. In 1842, Queen Victoria ordered a dessert service
comprising more than 200 pieces from Bloor Derby. It was
reported in the *Derby Mercury* that 'a splendid Dessert Service,

75

ordered by Her Majesty, may be seen in Mr. Bloor's warehouse, 34 Old Bond Street', during the week before Christmas, when it was due to be delivered. The display of the service attracted large crowds eager to see the plates, ice-pails and comports soon to grace the Queen's festive table.

In remembering the Christmas Day banquets held at Windsor before the death of Prince Albert, Queen Victoria wrote:

'At dinner there were all the Christmas dishes, of which we generally had to eat a little. First the cold baron of beef which stood on the large sideboard all decked out – brawn – game pies from Ireland and others – stuffed turkey – wild boar's head – which Albert was so fond of with a particular German sauce which the Coburg cook invented – mince pies etc. etc. – and then all sorts of Bonbons and figures and toys were brought at dessert, many of which were given to the children; and there used to be such great excitement and delight.'

Bloor Derby, *Comport and dessert plate*, porcelain with gilded decoration, 1841–2, RCINS 28568, 28569

Roast turkey first appeared at the Christmas feast table of Henry VIII and quickly became a popular festive dish. During Queen Victoria's long reign, roast or sometimes boiled turkey was either served as a *relevé* or was amongst the cold dishes on the sideboard, but was rarely the star of the banquet. This was the case on Christmas Day 1840, when it was just one of the 35 dishes served to Queen Victoria, Prince Albert and 17 guests at Windsor Castle. The menu also included turtle soup, roast swan à l'anglaise, iced knuckle of veal and hare curry. Carp, a traditional German Christmas dish, frequently appeared at the royal festive feast, particularly during the days of Prince Albert. It was customarily fished from a lake in Windsor Great Park.

The rise in popularity of turkey during the later nineteenth century can be attributed to the future Edward VII, for whom it was a personal favourite. It was among the principal dishes served at a lavish banquet hosted by the then Prince of Wales on Christmas Day 1875 aboard HMS *Serpis*, moored in Kolkata (formerly Calcutta). In the early twentieth century, turkey became the centrepiece of the Christmas meal, supplied for the royal table by one of the Sandringham Estate farms, a tradition which continues today.

Christmas pudding or plum pudding was not routinely served as part of the royal festive feast until the second half of the nineteenth century. However, its predecessor, plum broth, had been popular since the reign of Charles I and remained part of the royal Christmas Day meal until the early nineteenth century. George IV's royal plum broth, the recipe for which survives in the Royal Archives, contained beef and veal, as well as dried fruits, spices and large quantities of alcohol including port, brandy, madeira, sherry and

Minced Pyes distributed to His Royal Highness the Prince Regents Servants
on Christmas Day 1812 And on New Years Day 1813

1812   1813
Dec 25 Jan 1st

Lord Steward
Master of the Household
Gen.l Turner
Col.o Mc.Mahon
Col.l Bloomfield
S.r Gilbert Blane
Surgeon Phillips
Rich.d Walker Esq.r
Clerk Comptroller
1 Clerk of the Kitchen
2 d.o
3 d.o   d.o
Messenger
2 Master Cooks ea 4.o
Pastry Cook
2 Under Cooks ea 3
Roasting Cook
Women Cook
3 Boys ea 2
Kitchen Maid
2 Scullery Men ea 2
Confectioner
2.d d.o
2 Assistants ea 2
Gentleman of the Cellar
Yeo.o of the Cellar
Assistant d.o
Table Decker
Assistant d.o
Housekeeper
Coffee Room Maid
Assistant
6 Pages of the Back Stairs
4 Pages of the Presence
Serjeant Porter
Gentleman d.o
Assistant d.o
6 Messengers ea 1
Musical Page
Assistant d.o

Inspector of Househ.d deliveries
Clapasier
Household Laundress
Yeo.o of the Silver Scullery
2 Silver Scullery Men
2 d.o Women ea 2
10 Housemaids ea 1
10 Footmen ea 1
Steward
Grosvenor
Armory Man
Deadman
2 Pages Men ea 1
4 Porters at the Gate ea 2
4 Watchmen ea 1
3 Coal Porters ea 1
2 Lamp lighters ea 1
Gardener
Labourer in Trust
2 Carpenters ea 1
2 Bricklayers ea 1
Clerk of the Stables
Riding Master

Minced Pyes
Sent to Her Majesty
at Windsor

...Broth distributed to His Royal Highness the Prince Regent's Servants on [Ch]ristmas Day 1812 and on New Years Day 1813   141

List of royal household staff to be given plum broth and mince pies on Christmas and New Year's Day, 1812–13, Carlton House menu ledger, 1812–13, Royal Archives, RA MRH/MENUS/MAIN/MIXED/1 p. 141

claret. The broth would have been bright red in colour owing to the inclusion of ground cochineal. Throughout the reign of George IV it was traditional for members of the royal household to be given plum broth and mince pies on Christmas and New Year's Day.

In the reign of Queen Victoria, plum broth was replaced by plum pudding, though it did not become an integral part of the royal Christmas Day meal until the 1870s. By the late 1880s, Queen Victoria's chefs made more than 100 plum puddings to be dispatched as personal Christmas gifts to the Queen's closest relatives. The recipe, which made 300lb of pudding mixture, included 150 eggs, a whole bottle of rum and another of brandy, as well as four gallons of strong ale. This unusual ingredient gave the puddings a particular richness. It was among the ingredients for the 'Empire Christmas Pudding', which appeared on posters published by the Empire Marketing Board in 1929. The recipe, supplied by George V's chef Mr Cédard, used produce sourced from across the British Empire including Australian sultanas, Canadian flour, Jamaican rum and South African brandy.

Just as George IV had given plum broth to his staff over the festive season, Queen Victoria presented her household with plum puddings. This centuries-old tradition is continued today by The Queen and The Duke of Edinburgh, who each year give members of the Royal Household specially made Christmas puddings from Fortnum & Mason.

Opposite

Colonel Sir William James Colville (1827–1903), *Gentleman at a banquet*, watercolour, 1873, RCIN 928276

HRH The Duchess of York stirring Christmas pudding at a Training Hostel, Market Harborough, 1927

Plays, Pantos & Festive Entertainment

Since the Middle Ages, pageants, plays and masques have been performed at the royal court as part of the Christmas celebrations. The earliest recorded Christmas theatricals were staged at the court of Edward III (1312–77) and continue today, with pantomimes staged by the Royal Household at Windsor Castle. In a tradition dating back to the reign of Henry VIII, members of the royal family and even the monarch would take part in such Christmas festivities.

At the court of Henry VIII, lavish entertainments were performed during the Christmas celebrations beginning on Christmas Eve and continuing throughout the twelve days of Christmas until the feast of the Epiphany on 6 January. The festivities were presided over by the Lord of Misrule, who acted as a master of ceremonies. Appointed by the King, he was

We played & sang [...] & we had some dancing afterwards [...] Such a happy ending to the old year.
— Queen Victoria,
31 December 1841

Studio Lisa
(Lisa Sheridan)
(1894–1966),
*Princess Elizabeth
and Princess Margaret
performing in 'Old
Mother Red Riding
Boots'*, gelatin
silver print, 1944,
RCIN 2506250

adorned with ribbons, jewels and bells and followed by a procession of heralds, magicians, and fools in fancy dress. During the festive season, even the monarch had to obey the commands of the Lord of Misrule.

The festive entertainment commenced on Christmas Eve with a traditional 'mumming' or mimed folk play often telling the story of St George and the Dragon and including a personification of Christmas. The festivities would continue with a succession of spectacular pageants, masques, interludes, plays and musical performances devised by the Master of the Revels, the court official responsible for overseeing royal festivities and entertainment. On the night of Epiphany 1510, Richard Gibson, the recently appointed Master of the Revels, organised a magnificent pageant at Richmond Palace. Before the banquet began, a mountain, glistening with gold, set with stones, and topped by a golden tree hung with roses and pomegranates, was brought into the Great Hall. As it approached the King, a woman dressed in cloth of gold, followed by the children of honour, emerged from the mountain and performed a morris dance before the court.

The king would frequently take part in such entertainments himself. In 1511 Christmas was spent at Greenwich and, on New Year's Eve, a pageant called *Le Fortresse Dangerus* was held in which a castle, with gates, towers and a dungeon, was brought before the Queen, Catherine of Aragon. In the castle were six women 'clothed in Russet Satin, laide all ouer with leaues of Golde'. After it was drawn in, Henry and five male companions entered and attacked the castle, at the sight of which the women inside, apparently impressed by their gallantry, came down; all 12 danced together before the women led the men into the castle, which then 'sodainly vanished, out of their sightes'.

The festive entertainments ended that year on Twelfth Day with the King taking part in an Italian masque, 'a thing not seen afore in Englande'. Early court masques were distinct from pageants and other entertainments and involved a band of opulently masked and costumed people arriving unannounced after a feast to dance with the guests, before exiting again. After its arrival at the Tudor court, the masque and pageant became one, evolving into extravagant spectacles which combined music, dance, poetry and mime, set amongst elaborate moving scenery requiring complex mechanics and other special effects. The Christmas masque reached its height in the reign of James I and VI, when the court poet Ben Jonson and the architect and designer Inigo Jones collaborated on the production of these entertainments. Members of the royal family would frequently take part in masques, which were usually staged at the Banqueting House at Whitehall. On New Year's Day 1611, Henry Frederick, Prince of Wales (1594–1612) appeared in the title role of Jonson's masque *Oberon, the Faery Prince*, while his mother Anne of Denmark took part in at least five masques. In around 1610 the Queen was painted by the miniaturist Isaac Oliver in the elaborate costume she wore for a court masque.

Isaac Oliver (*c*.1565–1617), *Anne of Denmark* (1574–1619), watercolour on vellum laid on card, *c*.1610, RCIN 420025

85

Christmas theatricals, like Christmas itself, were banned under the Parliamentarians during the Commonwealth period; although they were revived at the Restoration court of Charles II, later entertainments never equalled those of earlier reigns.

At the Hanoverian courts of George I and George II (1683–1760), gambling was the most fashionable festive pastime in which the whole royal family would be involved. However, by the time of George III (1738–1820), theatrical performances were once again part of the royal Christmas celebrations, although now on a more domestic scale. In a letter to her son, William, Duke of Clarence, later William IV, Queen Charlotte described the festivities enjoyed by the royal family during Christmas 1782: 'the younger part of the family entertained us two evenings with a representation of several of Monsieur Gefsners (*sic*) idylls and two Pieces of Madame Genlis Theatre d'Education.'

During the reign of Queen Victoria, the Christmas pastimes enjoyed by the royal family were diverse; as in the days of her Tudor and Stuart predecessors, the festivities continued until at least Twelfth Night, which began with the arrival of the Twelfth Cake and usually ended with a game of snapdragon. In the early years of her reign, entertainments principally involved games like blind man's bluff and musical performances. On Christmas

First page of a letter from Queen Charlotte (1744–1818) to her son, William, Duke of Clarence, later William IV, 1782, Royal Archives, RA GEO/ADD/4/204/26

Ella Taylor (1827–1914), *Servants' children playing at blind man's bluff in the Hall*, ink and pencil, 5 January 1859, RCIN 918818

Eve 1842, the Queen and Prince Albert played Mendelssohn's *Symphony No. 3*, which the composer had sent the royal couple, knowing they were admirers of his work. After dinner, the Queen's band played Haydn's *Toy Symphony* for the assembled company. The Queen's performance of the same piece on Boxing Day the following year was described by her Maid of Honour Eleanor Stanley in a letter to her mother: 'yesterday evening we had a curious piece of music executed by the Queen's hand, to imitate the various sounds of penny trumpets, rattles, drums, and all sorts of toys, supposed to be Christmas gifts to the children of the family'.

Prince Albert was himself a talented composer. In her journal Queen Victoria records that on New Year's Eve 1841, the assembled

Ella Taylor (1827–1914), *After dinner at
Cambridge Cottage, Kew, Christmas 1858*,
pencil and watercolour, 1858, RCIN 918815

company 'played and sang some of dear Albert's songs'; two years later she wrote that the Prince spent the evening of Christmas Day 1843 composing a *Te Deum*, which he continued to work on until 27 January. It was performed on New Year's Day two years later when it was sung by the Queen's choristers with a full orchestral accompaniment to 'splendid effect'. The piece was publicly performed several times during the 1840s, and in 1850 Prince Albert published it, along with several others compositions. The Prince also composed a Christmas hymn in 1847, his handwritten version of which survives in one of two beautifully bound volumes in the Royal Library at Windsor.

Twelfth Night, which had formerly been one of the principal occasions for feasting and court entertainments, was celebrated on

Prince Albert (1819–61), *Te Deum*, manuscript, *c.*1843, RCIN 1077785

a less extravagant scale in the nineteenth century. However, Queen Victoria and her family continued the age-old festive tradition of the Twelfth Cake. The cake was traditionally served at the start of the Twelfth Night feast on 5 or 6 January. The original Twelfth Cake, served at the medieval and Tudor courts, took the form of bread similar to

Prince Albert (1819–61), *'Lebewohl': Wanderlied, with Christmas hymn and Die Winter Reise*, manuscript with watercolour frontispiece, 1853, RCIN 1077784

brioche, with dried fruit and spices. Central to the Twelfth Night celebration was the appointment of the King of the Bean, who was responsible for organising games and entertainments at the final festive feast. To select the King, a bean was baked inside the Twelfth Cake. Whoever received the slice containing the bean was 'crowned' the King of the Bean. At the court of Henry VIII it also became customary for a pea to be baked into the cake, and its discoverer would be declared Queen of the Pea.

In the early nineteenth century, the bean and the pea were replaced by silver trinkets such as thimbles or charms and the traditional fruited bread of the Middle Ages became fruit cake. Eighteenth- and nineteenth-century Twelfth Cakes were often elaborately decorated with sugar and almond paste, none more so than the royal Twelfth Cake. In 1849, the *Illustrated London News* published a description of Queen Victoria's 'superb' Twelfth Cake, alongside an engraving:

'The Cake was of regal dimensions, being about 30 inches in diameter, and tall in proportion: round the side the decorations consisted of strips of gilded paper, bowing outwards near the top, issuing from an elegant gold bordering. The figures, of which there were sixteen, on the top of the Cake, represented a party of beaux

Queen Victoria's Twelfth Cake, Illustrated London News, 13 January 1849

THE QUEEN'S TWELFTH CAKE.

and belles of the last century enjoying a repast al fresco, under some trees; whilst others, and some children, were dancing to minstrel strains. The repast, spread on the ground, with its full complements of comestibles, decanters, and wine-glasses […] was admirably modelled, as were also the figures, servants being represented handing refreshments to some of the gentlemen and ladies. […] The violinist and harpist seemed to be thoroughly impressed with the importance of their functions, and their characteristic attitudes were cleverly given. As a specimen of fancy workmanship, the ornaments to the cake do credit to the skill of Mr. Mawditt, the Royal confiseur.'

As new 'German' Christmas customs were embraced during the nineteenth century, the traditional Twelfth Night celebrations fell out of use. The Twelfth Cake was gradually replaced by the Christmas cake, while the charms hidden inside migrated to the Christmas pudding.

Queen Victoria was especially fond of the theatre, and the royal family would often attend a play during the Christmas season. On Boxing Day 1833, the then Princess Victoria went to Drury Lane Theatre to see a grand Christmas spectacle called *St George and the Dragon* or *The Seven Champions of Christendom*. The 14-year-old Princess vividly described the production in her journal, as well as making drawings of all the principal characters. St George, played by Andrew Ducrow, an equestrian circus performer, in particular captured her imagination: '[He] acted uncommonly well and rode beautifully. The horses were beautifully trained, and Mr. Ducrow's

Queen Victoria, when Princess Victoria of Kent, 1819–1901, *The combat between St George and the dragon*, pencil, watercolour and gold paint, 15 January 1834, RCIN 980015.fn

The combat between St George and
the Dragon. As Mr Ducrow
appeared on his horse at Drury
Lane in January 1834.

P.S. f. R.P.
Jan: 15th 1834

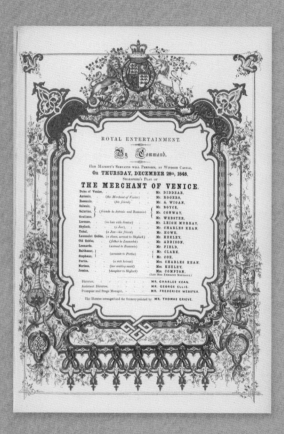

John Kemble Chapman (1795–1852), *Playbill for The Merchant of Venice from the court theatre, and royal dramatic record*, 1849, RCIN 970465

John Kemble Chapman (1795–1852), *Playbill for Hamlet from the court theatre, and royal dramatic record*, 1849, RCIN 970465

fight with the dragon, on horseback, was quite beautiful; the horse reared almost erect and never started or shied at the fiery dragon which came flapping and biting about him.'

After her marriage to Prince Albert and the birth of their children, Queen Victoria continued to enjoy visits to the theatre with her family. In 1850, she and the Prince Consort took their four children to Drury Lane to see the Christmas pantomime *Harlequin & good Queen Bess*. Describing the evening, the Queen wrote: 'The Clown, Mr Stilt, was wonderfully clever. The Children greatly enjoyed themselves.'

Between 1848 and 1861, plays were also frequently performed at Windsor Castle before the Queen and the assembled court at Christmas. The introduction of these performances, according to Queen Victoria, had been suggested by Prince Albert and necessitated the revival of the office of Master of the Revels. The Queen appointed the noted Shakespearian actor/manager Charles Kean as 'manager of the Christmas theatricals'. The first production, *The Merchant of Venice*, was staged on 28 December 1848; among the performers were Kean and his wife Ellen, also a celebrated actress. Queen Victoria described the event in her journal:

'We went to look at the preparation for the theatre & found all going on extremely well. At 8 we went over to the Rubens room. [...] The seats were extremely well arranged and on the platform which was up 3 steps, we two sat with Mama & the 4 Ladies & just behind us sat the company on seats raised one above the other, the company invited after dinner

had already taken their seats. The 3 children sat on the steps at our feet, half of our private band was stationed in the next room to our right, they played an Overture & also between the acts. The play was 'The merchant of Venice' & the beauties of the language were heard & understood as they hardly can be in a large theatre. Shakespeare's wit, his knowledge of human nature & of the character of man are unrivalled. I had never seen the play before, & much enjoyed it; there are such fine speeches in it. — It was a most successful performance & all acted well & in particular Charles Kean & Mrs. Kean, Mr. who is very gentlemanlike & quiet, besides Keeley (who was most laughable) & Mrs. Keeley. — The scenery was quite beautiful — all the dresses new, everything went so smoothly there was not a hitch of any kind; all this is dear Albert's own idea admirably carried out by Phipps & Charles Kean. One felt quite delighted & relieved as it was a nervous business & the difficulties very great.'

John Absolon (1815–95), 'The Merchant of Venice' as performed in the Rubens Room, Windsor Castle, before Queen Victoria, 28 December 1848, watercolour, 1848, RCIN 923591

Two weeks later, the assembled company was this time treated to a
performance of *Hamlet*, with the title role played by Charles Kean.
The production was again staged in the Rubens Room (or King's
Drawing Room), and was recorded in a watercolour by John Absolon.

 Queen Victoria delighted in performances of many kinds,
but her particular favourite was a variation on charades known as
tableaux vivants. These involved actors arranged in static poses,
usually in full costume and with props and scenery, to represent a
specific scene or incident. At Queen Victoria's court, the performers
were usually the royal children. In later years, when Christmas was

John Absolon
(1815–95), *'Hamlet' as
performed in the Rubens
Room, Windsor Castle,
before Queen Victoria,
11 January 1849*,
watercolour, 1849,
RCIN 923589

spent at Osborne, the Queen's youngest child Princess Beatrice, who
continued to live with her mother even after her marriage, took a
starring role in the annual tableaux. Describing the entertainments
staged in 1888, Queen Victoria wrote:

> 'The Tableaux were quite beautiful & so well arranged. After
> the Band playing a short overture, the curtain rose slowly, &
> brought the Queen of Sheba before Solomon, to view. Beatrice
> looked very well in this, in real Eastern draperies, India shawls,
> & jewels. Sir H. Ponsonby was admirable as Solomon. The

Byrne & Co. (active
late 1870s–1900s),
*'Queen of Sheba' from an
album of photographs of
tableaux vivants staged
at Osborne, 7–10 January
1888*, albumen print,
1888, RCIN 2913350

curtain rose 3 times, & the poses were slightly altered. The
Band played again for ¼ of an hour, & the curtain rose on a
scene in 'Carmen', the music of the charming Opera being
played to it. Liko as Toreador (looking very handsome), Minnie
Cochrane as Carmen, & Major Bigge as the jealous Don Josè,
were admirable. The 3rd Tableau, & in some ways perhaps, the
finest, was the statue scene from Shakespeare's 'Winter's Tale'
[…] The 4th Tableau represented Queen Elisabeth & Sir Walter
Raleigh. Beatrice was wonderfully well got up like the pictures
of Queen Elisabeth. Liko took the part of Sir W. Raleigh, &
Mr Yorke that of Ld Leicester. When this was over, Beatrice,
Liko, & the others sat with us to the last Tableau
'Homage', which was a very unexpected surprise. My
bust being wreathed with flowers stood in the centre,
& ladies were grouped round below it. The Band
played 'Home, sweet Home'. This brought to a close,
what really were lovely Tableaux & a great treat.'

In 1892, the tableaux spelled out the words 'New
Year', with each scene representing a different
letter, chosen by Queen Victoria. Rehearsals for
tableaux vivants typically went on for days before
the performance, which might be repeated several
times over the festive period, and guests would be
specially invited to see them. On several occasions
during the 1880s and '90s, the festive tableaux were
photographed for posterity. On one occasion the

Queen Victoria
(1819–1901), *List
of guests at a tableaux
vivants performance,
8 January 1891,*
Royal Archives,
RA VIC/MAIN/QVJ/
1892 8 January

Gustav William
Henry Mullins
(1854–1921),
*'Christmas' from an
album of 20 hand-
coloured photographs
of tableaux vivants of
historical events staged
by members of the royal
family at Balmoral
Castle and Osborne,*
overpainted albumen
print, 1890–93,
RCIN 2508872

last tableaux represented Christmas and included the figure of
Father Christmas, and a chef arriving with the traditional boar's
head. In her journal, the 75-year-old Queen Victoria complained
that she could no longer see well enough to watch the tableaux
without the aid of opera glasses.

In the wartime years of the early 1940s, Her Majesty The Queen
(then Princess Elizabeth) and her sister Princess Margaret (1930–
2002) took part in a series of Christmas pantomimes intended to
raise money for charity. Performers included local children, some
of them evacuees, and friends of the Princesses, with occasional
help from service personnel based in the Windsor area. In 1942,
a production of *Sleeping Beauty* was staged at Windsor Castle in
which the then 16-year-old Princess Elizabeth took the role of the

101

Prince, appearing in a white satin costume and white wig during the second act. Princess Margaret played Thistledown, the principal fairy, while other members of the royal family, including the Princesses' cousins the Duke of Kent (b.1935) and Princess Alexandra (b.1936) also took parts.

In 1943, the pantomime was *Aladdin*, written and produced, as it had been the year before, by Hubert Tanner, Headmaster of the Royal School at Windsor. That year, the future Queen took the title role, while Princess Margaret played the part of Princess Roxana. Costumes were supplied by the court costumier and theatrical dress

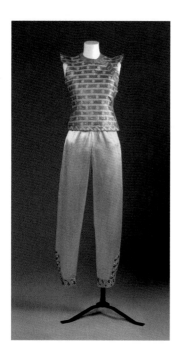

Left

Jacket and long dress worn by Princess Margaret as Princess Roxana in 'Aladdin' at Windsor Castle, embroidered silk, 1943, RCIN 70778

Far left

Tunic and trousers worn by Princess Elizabeth, later Queen Elizabeth II, in 'Aladdin' at Windsor Castle, embroidered satin and silk, 1943, RCIN 70779

maker L. & H. Nathan Ltd. Princess Elizabeth's
costumes included cream satin pantaloons and a
sleeveless silk top and a three-piece outfit comprising
a gold brocade jacket with elaborate frog fastenings,
a matching hat with a silk tassel, and a pair of
turquoise dungarees. For her role, Princess Margaret
wore a red and gold embroidered dress and matching
jacket with frog fastenings. The performance
included topical references, including teasing inside

Studio Lisa (Lisa Sheridan)
(1894–1966), *Princess Elizabeth,*
later Queen Elizabeth II, and
Princess Margaret with friends in
'Sleeping Beauty', in the Waterloo
Chamber at Windsor Castle, gelatin
silver print, 1942, RCIN 2085811

jokes directed at various members of the royal household and the artist Gerald Kelly, who had been slow in producing the official state portraits of King George VI and Queen Elizabeth. The pantomime was attended that year by Prince Philip, who was at Windsor for Christmas.

The final pantomime, staged in 1944, was devised by the Princesses, then aged 18 and 14, with the help of Hubert Tanner. *Old Mother Red Riding Boots* was an original combination of the best parts of many pantomimes. The production was staged, as in previous years, in the Waterloo Chamber at Windsor Castle. The sets in 1944 were designed by the Academy Award-winning MGM art director Vincent Korda. Part of the scenery included the so-called 'pantomime pictures', which were hung in the frames left empty after Thomas Lawrence's Waterloo Commission portraits had been removed for safe-keeping at the beginning of the war. The 'pantomime pictures' were never taken down and they continue to hang behind Lawrence's portraits in the Waterloo Chamber.

Studio Lisa (Lisa Sheridan) (1894–1966), *Princess Elizabeth, later Queen Elizabeth II, and Princess Margaret in 'Aladdin' at Windsor Castle*, gelatin silver print with gold toning, 1943, RCIN 2813938

Studio Lisa (Lisa
Sheridan) (1894–1966),
*Princess Elizabeth, later
Queen Elizabeth II
in 'Old Mother Red
Riding Boots'*, gelatin
silver print, 1944,
RCIN 2506246

The 'pantomime pictures', Waterloo Chamber, Windsor Castle, gelatin silver print, 1943, RCIN 2808501

Old Mother Red Riding Boots, in which Princess Elizabeth played the part of Lady Christina Sherwood and Princess Margaret appeared as the Honourable Lucinda Fairfax, was performed on four consecutive nights between 20 and 23 December. On the first night, tickets for just one shilling were reserved for members of the royal household, while on the three following nights tickets were sold for between 2 shillings and 6 pence, roughly £4.40 today, and 7 shillings and 6 pence, equal to around £13.30. Including the sale of souvenir programmes and additional donations, the pantomime raised £293 and 19 shillings, approximately £10,450 in today's money. Proceeds went to the Wool Fund, which supplied knitting wool for the making of comforters for the armed forces.

Although members of the Royal Family no longer perform, plays and pantomimes are still staged in the Waterloo Chamber at Windsor Castle over the festive period, with performances for both employees of the Royal Household and the general public.

Studio Lisa (Lisa Sheridan) (1894–1966), *Cast of 'Old Mother Red Riding Boots'*, gelatin silver print, 1944, RCIN 2506225

Snow Sports & Winter Activities

NOW SPORTS AND OTHER OUTDOOR WINTER ACTIVITIES HAVE LONG BEEN FASHIONABLE ROYAL PASTIMES. BETWEEN THE SEVENTEENTH AND EARLY NINETEENTH CENTURIES, SOMETIMES CALLED THE 'LITTLE ICE AGE', THE RIVER THAMES WOULD OCCASIONALLY FREEZE OVER IN THE WINTER MONTHS.

On one such occasion in 1536, it is recorded that Henry VIII travelled from the Palace of Whitehall to his residence at Greenwich by sleigh, over the frozen river. When the Thames froze again in winter 1564, Elizabeth I (1533–1603) frequently took to the ice to 'shoot at marks' (archery). In December 1683, when the Thames froze solid for two months, a frost fair was set up on the ice between London Bridge and Temple. Entertainments included sledging, ice skating, horse and coach races and puppet shows. On 31 February 1684, the fair was attended by Charles II and his Queen, Catherine of Braganza (1638–1705).

There is always something peculiarly bright & cheery in winter amusements.
— QUEEN VICTORIA,
12 DECEMBER 1844

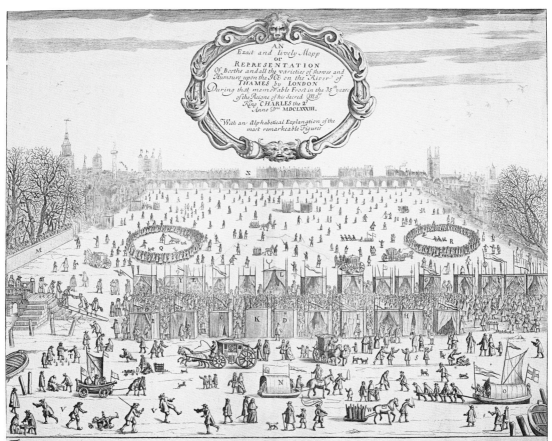

An Exact and Lively Mapp or Representation of Booths and all the
varieties of shows and humours upon the Ice of the River of Thames
by London, 1684, etching and engraving, 1684, RCIN 750170

Drawn by J.Burnett.

112

After John Burnett (1784–1868), *Skating in St James's Park before Buckingham House*, hand-coloured lithograph, 1817, RCIN 702801

Londoners had enjoyed skating on frozen lakes and occasionally on the Thames for centuries, but ice skating was to become a craze in the capital in the eighteenth and nineteenth centuries. 1816, known as the 'Year Without a Summer', was unseasonably cold, and the canal in St James's Park froze over several times. On 1 December that year, the ice was reported to be 'exceedingly crowded with skaters'. A print published a month later, on 2 January 1817, shows skaters on the ice in front of Buckingham Palace, then Buckingham House, with the royal coach approaching from the right, followed by a mounted guard.

Prince Albert was an accomplished and enthusiastic skater and frequently went skating on the frozen lake at Frogmore and in the gardens at Buckingham Palace. Queen Victoria, although she did not skate herself, enjoyed watching her husband on the ice. She wrote in her journal for 31 December 1846: 'Albert went down to Frogmore to skate, & I joined him there later with Vicky, the Dss of Sutherland & Ly Douro. It was very pleasant down there, & the whole, a gay sight. Albert skates so beautifully, & always is the winner at the games of hockey.'

113

On 9 February 1841, while skating in the gardens at Buckingham Palace, Prince Albert fell through the ice; skating fatalities were not uncommon and, in her journal, the Queen described the scene and her terror at the danger to her beloved Albert:

'Albert put on his skates, & helped me to walk across the ice, which was very smooth & hard, — to the island. He skated all round the Lake, & on coming close to the bridge, — quite a narrow place, I, standing alone on the bank, — said, 'it is unsafe here', & no sooner had I said this, than the ice cracked, & Albert was in the water up to his head, even for a moment below. In my agony of fright & despair, I screamed, & stretched out my arm. [...] My dearest Albert managed to catch my arm, & reached the ground in safety. Oh! how thankful I felt to see him at my side again & that God should have mercifully preserved him from such a great danger! He cut his chin a little, & was of course dripping with water, so that he ran home as fast as he could. It was a horrid experience, & I never felt anything so dreadful, as seeing my beloved one in the water, & thinking, as I did, that I should lose him before my very eyes unable to rescue him! [...] When I got home, I found Albert running about to warm himself & looking very pale. He took a hot bath & went to bed for a bit, well wrapped up.'

The Prince recounted the tale himself in a letter to his adoptive grandmother Caroline, Duchess of Saxe-Gotha-Altenburg (1771–1848), commending his wife as 'the only person who had the presence of mind to lend me assistance'. These sentiments were reiterated when the story was widely reported in newspapers around the world, Queen Victoria being applauded for having 'manifested the greatest courage upon the occasion, and acted with the most intrepid coolness'.

By the mid-nineteenth century, skating was so popular that attempts were being made to produce artificial ice so that the pastime could be enjoyed all year round. In 1843 an artificial ice rink opened at the Baker Street Bazaar. The 'Glaciarium' featured a 3,000 square foot rink with a backdrop of painted alpine scenery and featured live music to skate to, courtesy of the resident 'promenade band'. Shortly after the opening it was reported in the *Illustrated London News* that Prince Albert had visited the Glaciarium to skate and declared his intention of going again.

Queen Victoria in a sledge and Prince Albert skating at Frogmore, colour relief half-tone, 1880–1900, RCIN 605929

Though Queen Victoria took instruction in skating from Mr Talbot, a tutor from Eton, she preferred to be pushed around the ice in a sledge. Describing her first foray onto the ice on 30 December 1840, the Queen wrote: 'We drove down to Frogmore & Albert pushed me in a sledge chair on the ice, which was delightful, & it went with such rapidity. I had never been on the ice before.'

The royal children were unsurprisingly enthusiastic participants in this winter fun. In her journal Queen Victoria recounted an occasion in February 1853 when, having stayed on at Windsor after Christmas,

'Albert & the 4 girls tried a little sledge, a kind of bob sleigh, up & down the bank from the Terrace, where there was still a good deal of snow left & they went down beautifully, to their great delight, — like on a 'Montagne Russe' [roller-coaster]. The Boys joined later. Albert says it is the great amusement of grown-ups, as well as children, in Germany.'

Above

J. Gilfoy, *Design for Queen Victoria's sledge*, watercolour on board, *c*.1844, Science Museum, London

Left

Prince Albert (1819–61) (designer), Hooper & Co. (maker), *Queen Victoria's sledge*, *c*.1844, Royal Mews

THE ROYAL CHILDREN'S SLEDGE.

The royal children's sledge,
Illustrated London News,
1854, RCIN 700779

Queen Victoria was also fond of sleigh riding, especially when
staying at Brighton and Windsor. Her sledge was painted
in red and gold, lined with crimson velvet and decorated
with plumes of ostrich feathers. It had been designed by
Prince Albert and built under his direction by the carriage-
maker Hooper & Co. A design for the sledge survives in the
Science Museum, London, while the sledge itself is housed
at the Royal Mews, Windsor. The royal children also had a
smaller sledge, pulled by a single pony.

On one occasion in February 1845, when the royal family
were staying at the Royal Pavilion, Brighton, it began to
snow heavily, and a special messenger was sent to Windsor

with instructions that the royal sleigh and ponies be brought
to Brighton without delay. A newspaper account told how the
Queen, accompanied by the dowager Lady Lyttelton, who had the
Princess Royal in her arms, rode out in the sledge as far as Clayton
Tunnel. In her journal, the Queen described the day:

> 'At 3 o'clock we went out in it [the sledge] together &
> I thought it quite charming. [...] The horses with their
> handsome red harness & many bells, had a charming effect.
> Albert drove from the seat. We went along the London road,
> a good way beyond Patcham, & the sledge went delightfully
> though the road was unfortunately very
> much broken up in places, but in others
> it was covered with snow. The bright blue
> sky & sunshine, together with the sound
> of the bells, had a very exhilarating effect.
> We came home even faster than we went,
> & the air was intensely cold. Our 2 dear
> ponies 'Keith' & 'Kintore' went so well.'

Such winter activities were enjoyed by the
entire royal family, particularly during the
festive period spent at Windsor Castle. As
well as regular skating parties, games of ice
hockey on the frozen lake at Frogmore,
referred to by Queen Victoria as the
'skating pond', were a frequent occurrence

Monogrammist
JWG (active 1845)
after B. Herring
Junior, *Prince Albert
driving the Queen and
Princess Royal in their
sledge, at Brighton*,
lithograph printed in
colour with hand-
colouring, *c.*1845,
RCIN 605915

Prince Albert driving the Queen & Princess Royal in

Princess Victoria of Wales (1868–1935), *Prince Albert, later King George VI, and Princess Mary playing ice hockey*, platinum and gelatin silver prints mounted on card, *c.*1904–5, RCIN 2923705

ledge, at Brighton.

over the festive season. On New Year's Eve 1853, the royal family took part in such a hockey game:

'I went with the Children, down to the Skating Pond, where we went in chairs, & tried to push ourselves along, with spiked poles. The Children all got on very well. At 3 we all went down to the ice, where were assembled all the Gentlemen & at least 7 or 8 Officers. The Band was playing in a small island in the centre of the pond. The games [hockey] were extremely animated. Before they began all the Children, & we ladies, were driven about in chairs, which is always delightful. The Boys always join in the game & are most active, never minding how many falls they get. We remained till ½ p. 4, & it was a most gay & pretty scene. Mulled wine is always served afterwards in the Orangery.'

During the winter of 1842 Victoria and Albert travelled from Windsor, where they had celebrated Christmas, to Claremont in Surrey. In the course of their stay, the royal couple amused themselves by building a huge snowman, with the assistance of the gardener and five other men from the estate. Writing in her journal, the Queen noted that it was at least 12 feet high and the first snowman she had ever seen. The building of a more diminutive snowman on New Year's Day 1861 by a party including Queen Victoria's cousin, Princess Mary Adelaide of Cambridge (1833–97), is recorded in a watercolour by Cambridge family friend Ella Taylor.

Ella Taylor (1827–1914), *Princess Mary Adelaide of Cambridge and John du Plat Taylor making a snowman*, pencil and watercolour with touches of bodycolour on paper, 1861, RCIN 918825

Queen Victoria's children continued to enjoy winter sports and activities with their own families. The Prince and Princess of Wales, later King Edward VII and Queen Alexandra, went skating or sledging on the lake at Sandringham, when the weather permitted, while younger members of the Wales family enjoyed snowball fights on the Estate. A drawing by Karl Wilhelm Friedrich Bauerle shows the Prince of Wales pushing his four eldest children in a sledge, while Princess Alexandra skates nearby.

In 1874, the Prince and Princess of Wales travelled to St Petersburg for the wedding of the Prince's younger brother Alfred, Duke of Edinburgh, to the Grand Duchess Marie (1853–1920), daughter of Tsar Alexander II of Russia (1818–81).

Colonel Sir William James Colville (1827–1903), *Revd William Lake Onslow with Prince Albert Victor and Prince George*, pencil and watercolour on paper, 1874, RCIN 928378

Carl Wilhelm Friedrich Bauerle (1831–1912), *The Prince of Wales and his family on the ice at Sandringham*, pencil, grey wash and pen and ink, 1871, RCIN 451938

During the visit, the Prince and Princess of Wales joined a skating party, which included the bride and groom, as well as the future Tsar Alexander III (1845–94). The artist Nicholas Chevalier had accompanied the British royal party to St Petersburg and, at the request of the Prince of Wales, made a number of drawings of the royals skating.

In late 1869, Queen Victoria's third son Prince Arthur, Duke of Connaught and Strathearn (1850–1942), was in Canada with his regiment, the First Battalion of the Rifle Brigade, which was then stationed in Montreal. During his stay, the Prince enjoyed winter sports including skating and sledging. In early 1870, a fancy-dress skating carnival was held at the Victoria Rink, Montreal, in honour of Prince Arthur, who went dressed as Charles I. The event was attended by hundreds of skaters, many in costume or military dress. The arena itself was decked with evergreen boughs and flags.

In 1890, Prince Arthur and his family spent Christmas with Queen Victoria at Osborne House on the Isle of Wight.

Opposite

Attributed to Princess Louise Margaret, Duchess of Connaught (1860–1917), *Princess Patricia and Princess Margaret of Connaught with Victoria Bigge*, gelatin silver print, 1890–91, RCIN 2801316

Below

Nicholas Chevalier (1828–1902), *People skating in St Petersburg*, pencil on paper, 1874, RCIN 926273

Here, too, there was a lake which would sometimes freeze over; during their stay, the Connaughts, including eight-year-old Princess Margaret (1882–1920) and four-year-old Princess Patricia (1886–1974), enjoyed skating and sledging. After moving to Canada in 1911, when Prince Arthur was made Governor-General, the family continued to enjoy regular skating in the winter months.

Left

William Notman (1826–91), *Prince Arthur skating in Canada*, albumen print, January 1870, RCIN 2902195

Right

William Notman (1826–91), *Prince Arthur, Colonel Howard Elphinstone and Lt Arthur Pickard, Canada*, albumen print, 1870, RCIN 2902200

The lake at Sandringham froze again in the winter of 1907–8, and over the festive period the Prince of Wales, later King George V, enjoyed skating with his family, just as he had done with his parents in the previous century. The younger generation of the Wales family, including 14-year-old Prince Edward, later Edward VIII, recycled the 'Sandringham 1871' sledge used by their grandfather King Edward VII to push his young family around the ice almost four decades earlier.

Left

The Wales family skating at Sandringham, gelatin silver print pasted onto card, 5 January 1908, RCIN 2303331

Above

The Duke and Duchess of Connaught and Princess Patricia skating with two companions, gelatin silver print, 1912, RCIN 2922208

125

THE CHRISTMAS BROADCAST

OR MANY PEOPLE ACROSS BRITAIN AND THE COMMONWEALTH, THE QUEEN'S ANNUAL CHRISTMAS BROADCAST IS AN INTEGRAL PART OF THE CHRISTMAS DAY FESTIVITIES. THE FIRST CHRISTMAS BROADCAST WAS MADE BY KING GEORGE V ON CHRISTMAS DAY 1932.

However, the idea of a Christmas message from the sovereign had first been proposed a decade earlier, when John Reith, the founding father and first Director-General of the BBC approached the King about making a short broadcast on the newly created radio service. The King initially declined, believing radio to be reserved for entertainment and political broadcasting. When, ten years later, Reith again suggested a royal Christmas broadcast as a way to inaugurate the new Empire Service (now the World Service), George V somewhat reluctantly agreed, encouraged by his wife, Queen Mary, and the Prime Minister, Ramsay MacDonald. The King was understandably

… wherever and however you are watching or listening, I wish you a peaceful and very happy Christmas.
— HM THE QUEEN,
25 DECEMBER 2017

The Times, *King George V making his Christmas broadcast,*
photographic print on card, 1934, RCIN 2108165

hesitant about using the relatively untested medium of radio in this way, but, after a reassuring visit to the BBC in the summer of 1932, he agreed to make the broadcast.

The speech was to form the climax of an hour-long programme of seasonal greetings from around the world, beginning in London and taking in Cardiff, Belfast, Edinburgh, Dublin, Halifax (Nova Scotia), Montreal, Winnipeg, Vancouver, Wellington, Sydney, Brisbane, Cape Town, Gibraltar and finally Sandringham, where the royal family traditionally spent Christmas. A temporary studio was set up in a small office formerly used by the King's Private Secretary, Francis Knollys. In order for the transmission to reach countries across the world, the microphones at Sandringham were connected through Post Office land-lines to the control room at BBC Broadcasting House. From there a connection was made to BBC transmitters in the Home Service and to the Empire Broadcasting Station at Daventry, which had six short-wave transmitters. The General Post Office was used to reach Australia, Canada, India, Kenya and South Africa. The hour of the broadcast – 3pm – was chosen as the best time for reaching as many countries as possible using short waves from transmitters in Britain. In the event the speech began at 3:05pm.

Prior to the broadcast, King George V carried out several voice tests to determine where best to position the table upon which the microphones would be placed. He was also instructed on the use of the cue-light, which signalled when the transmission was 'on air'; other than this and a warning about the dangers of ambient noise such as rustling papers, the King was given no further training.

The speech itself, consisting of fewer than 300 words and lasting only two and a half minutes, had been painstakingly drafted by the King with the help of his friend, the writer Rudyard Kipling. The speech focused on the advances in technology that permitted the King to deliver a message to all parts of the world, and infinite care had been taken to use straightforward, accessible language which could be easily understood.

'Through one of the marvels of modern Science, I am enabled, this Christmas Day, to speak to all my peoples throughout the Empire. I take it as a good omen that Wireless should have reached its present perfection at a time when the Empire has been linked in closer union. For it offers us immense possibilities to make that union closer still.

It may be that our future may lay upon us more than one stern test. Our past will have taught us how to meet it unshaken. For the present, the work to which we are all equally bound is to arrive at a reasoned tranquillity within our borders; to regain prosperity without self-seeking; and to carry with us those whom the burden of past years has disheartened or overborne.

My life's aim has been to serve as I might, towards those ends. Your loyalty, your confidence in me has been my abundant reward.

I speak now from my home and from my heart to you all. To men and women so cut off by the snows, the desert or the sea that only voices out of the air can reach them; to those cut off from fuller life by blindness, sickness, or infirmity; and to those who are celebrating this day with their children and grand-children. To all – to each – I wish a Happy Christmas. God Bless You!'

The broadcast was heard by more than 20 million people around the
world, including a congregation assembled in St Paul's Cathedral
and other members of the royal family at Sandringham, who
gathered to listen to the radio. An article published two days later
in *The Times* called the King's speech the most notable event of
Christmastime, while the *Cape Times* of Cape Town described it
as 'a truly remarkable event […] that posterity will look back upon
it as a landmark of human progress'. The King himself wrote to
congratulate John Reith on the success of the broadcast.

Peter North,
*King George VI
Making a Radio
Broadcast*,
photographic
print, 1937,
RCIN 2809742

King George V broadcast a speech on the Empire Service every
Christmas for the rest of his life, though his personal diaries suggest
he found it an ordeal. After the broadcast of Christmas Day 1934
the King wrote, 'At 3.30 I broadcasted my message to the Empire,
very glad when it was over.' That year, the King was introduced
by Walter Walton Handy, a 65-year-old
shepherd from Warwickshire, whose words
were complemented by carol singers and
the ringing of church bells. George V's last
Christmas message was broadcast in 1935,
less than a month before his death.

King George VI broadcast his first
Christmas speech from Sandringham on
Christmas Day 1937. In it, he thanked the
nation and Empire for their support during
his first year on the throne. Though by this
time the Christmas broadcast had already
proved very popular, it had not yet become

British Broadcasting
Corporation,
*King George VI making
his Christmas broadcast,*
photographic print,
25 December 1944,
RCIN 2000796

a regular tradition and there was no broadcast in 1938. It was the outbreak of World War Two in 1939 that firmly established the Royal Christmas Broadcast as an annual event. That year, the King, dressed in the uniform of the Admiral of the Fleet, having resolved not to wear civilian clothes while the war continued, sat before two microphones and addressed the Empire:

'The festival which we all know as Christmas is, above all, the festival of peace and of the home. Among all free peoples the love of peace is profound, for this alone gives security to the home. But true peace is in the hearts of men, and it is the tragedy of this time that there are powerful countries whose whole direction and policy are based on aggression and the suppression of all that we hold dear for mankind.

It is this that has stirred our peoples and given them a unity unknown in any previous way. We feel in our hearts that we are fighting against wickedness, and this conviction will give us strength from day to day to persevere until victory is assured.'

After expressing his pride in the Royal Navy, the Mercantile Marine, the Air Force and the armies of the Empire and his gratitude for their service and self-sacrifice, the King continued:

'Such is the spirit of the Empire, of the great Dominions, of India, of every Colony, large or small. From all alike have come offers of help for which the Mother Country can never be sufficiently grateful. Such unity in aim and in effort has never been seen in the world before. I believe from my heart that the cause which binds together my peoples and our gallant and faithful Allies is the cause of Christian civilization. On no other basis can a true civilization be built. Let us remember this through the dark times ahead of us and when we are making the peace for which all men pray.

A new year is at hand. We cannot tell which it will bring. If it brings peace how thankful we shall all be. If it brings continued struggle, we shall remain undaunted. In the meantime, I feel that we may all find a message of encouragement in the lines which, in my closing words, I would like to say to you:

I said to the man

who stood at the gate of the year,

"Give me a light that I may tread safely into the unknown."

And he replied,

"Go out into the darkness

and put your hand into the hand of God.

That shall be to you

better than light

and safer than a known way!"

May that Almighty hand guide and uphold us all.'

Despite the King's lack of enthusiasm for the task – he wrote in his diary that it was 'always an ordeal for me & I don't begin to enjoy Christmas until after it is over' – the 1939 speech was a landmark in the history of the Christmas broadcast. In tune with the prevailing mood of the moment, the King's speech had an important effect on the listening public as they were plunged into the uncertainty of war. The BBC was inundated with enquiries about the poem read by the King at the close of the speech. The lines had been brought to the attention of King George VI by the Queen, who had read them in *The Times*, where the quotation had been published anonymously. The author, Minnie Louise Haskins, a writer, academic and social welfare promoter, had not heard the Christmas Day broadcast, but recognised the lines on hearing a summary of the speech on Boxing Day. The poem has had lasting royal associations. It is inscribed on a panel affixed to the gates of the George VI Memorial Chapel in

Opposite

Planet News Ltd,
*HM Queen Elizabeth II
making her first
Christmas broadcast*,
gelatin silver print,
25 December 1952,
RCIN 2004814

St George's Chapel, Windsor, and it was read at the State Funeral of Queen Elizabeth The Queen Mother in 2002, as well as at the unveiling of her statue near Buckingham Palace in 2009.

King George VI continued to make yearly Christmas broadcasts throughout the war and for the rest of his life. His final speech, the first to be pre-recorded owing to the King's uncertain health, was broadcast on Christmas Day 1951, just weeks before his death.

Her Majesty The Queen delivered her first Christmas message to the Commonwealth from her study at Sandringham on 25 December 1952. In a BBC report, it was noted that she used the same desk and chair as had been used by both her father and grandfather.

'Each Christmas, at this time, my beloved father broadcast a message to his people in all parts of the world. To-day I am doing this to you, who are now my people. As he used to do, I am speaking to you from my own home, where I am spending Christmas with my family; and let me say at once how I hope that your children are enjoying themselves as much as mine are on a day which is especially the children's festival, kept in honour of the Child born at Bethlehem nearly two thousand years ago.

Most of you to whom I am speaking will be in your own homes, but I have a special thought for those who are serving their country in distant lands far from their families. Wherever you are, either at home or away, in snow or in sunshine, I give you my affectionate greetings, with every good wish for Christmas and the New Year.

At Christmas our thoughts are always full of our homes and our families. This is the day when members of the same family

try to come together, or if separated by distance or events meet
in spirit and affection by exchanging greetings. But we belong,
you and I, to a far larger family. We belong, all of us, to the
British Commonwealth and Empire, that immense union of
nations, with their homes set in all the four corners of the earth.
Like our own families, it can be a great power for good – a force
which I believe can be of immeasurable benefit to all humanity.

My father, and my grandfather before him, worked all their lives
to unite our peoples ever more closely, and to maintain its ideals
which were so near to their hearts. I shall strive to carry on their
work. Already you have given me strength to do so. For, since my
accession ten months ago, your loyalty and affection have been an
immense support and encouragement. I want to take this Christmas
Day, my first opportunity, to thank you with all my heart […]

At my Coronation next June, I shall dedicate myself
anew to your service. I shall do so in the presence of a great
congregation, drawn from every part of the Commonwealth and
Empire, while millions outside Westminster Abbey will hear the
promises and the prayers being offered up within its walls, and
see much of the ancient ceremony in which Kings and Queens
before me have taken part through century upon century.

You will be keeping it as a holiday; but I want to ask you all,
whatever your religion may be, to pray for me on that day – to
pray that God may give me wisdom and strength to carry out
the solemn promises I shall be making, and that I may faithfully
serve Him and you, all the days of my life.

May God bless and guide you all through the coming year.'

Central Press Photos Ltd., *HM Queen Elizabeth II making her first televised Christmas broadcast*, gelatin silver print, 25 December 1957, RCIN 2507994

The Queen has made a Christmas broadcast each year throughout her reign, with the exception of 1969 when a documentary, *Royal Family*, aired over the festive period. Such was the public concern at this apparent break with tradition that Her Majesty The Queen issued a written message of reassurance that the broadcast would return the following year, so integral to Christmas had it become.

The first televised Royal Christmas Message was broadcast live on Christmas Day 1957, the twenty-fifth anniversary of King George V's first radio broadcast. In a speech written with the assistance of The Duke of Edinburgh, The Queen noted the milestone and the advance of technology, which allowed viewers to see her in her own home, decorated for Christmas like many millions of homes across the world:

'Happy Christmas.

Twenty-five years ago my grandfather broadcast the first of these Christmas messages. Today is another landmark because television has made it possible for many of you to see me in your homes on Christmas Day. My own family often gather round to watch television as they are this moment, and that is how I imagine you now. I very much hope that this new medium will make my Christmas message more personal and direct.

It is inevitable that I should seem a rather remote figure to many of you. A successor to the Kings and Queens of history; someone whose face may be familiar in newspapers and films but who never really touches your personal lives. But now at least for a few minutes I welcome you to the peace of my own home.'

After reading a few lines from John Bunyan's *Pilgrim's Progress*, the Queen concluded her speech with some final good wishes:

'I hope that 1958 may bring you God's blessing and all the things you long for.

And so I wish you all, young and old, wherever you may be, all the fun and enjoyment, and the peace of a very happy Christmas.'

The broadcast was watched by 16.5 million people around the world.

Since 1960, broadcasts have been recorded in advance in order that copies can be sent around the world to the Commonwealth nations to be broadcast at a convenient local time. The message is recorded a few days before Christmas, and filming usually takes place at Buckingham Palace, though recordings have also been made at Windsor Castle and at Sandringham. In 1975, the Christmas broadcast was filmed outdoors for the first time, in the gardens of Buckingham Palace. Until 1996, the Queen's Christmas message was always produced by the BBC, but since 1997 the BBC and ITV have alternated filming and production every two years; beginning in 2011, Sky News was added to this rotation. In the year of Her Majesty's Diamond Jubilee in 2012, the Christmas broadcast was recorded in 3D for the first time.

HM Queen Elizabeth II makes her Christmas broadcast, Buckingham Palace, 1975, RCIN 2004805

Planning for the broadcast begins months in advance, when the Queen decides on the themes she wishes to address. The broadcast has been and remains the monarch's own personal message to the nation and Commonwealth. Typically it reflects current issues and events, as well as the sovereign's own personal milestones and feelings on Christmas. Since its inception in 1932, the broadcast has acted as a chronicle of global, national and personal events which have affected both the monarch and their audience. It continues to be an integral part of Christmas Day for millions of people around the world.

HM Queen Elizabeth II makes her Christmas Broadcast, 2017

ACKNOWLEDGEMENTS

For their help in the preparation of this book, I would like to
express my thanks to my colleagues in the Royal Household:
to Allison Derret and Bill Stocking of the Royal Archives; to
Paul Stonell and Catlin Langford of the Photograph Library; to
Elizabeth Clark Ashby and Emma Stuart of the Royal Library;
to Agata Rutkowska and Eva Zielinska-Millar of the Image
Library and to Elizabeth Silverton, Rosie Bick and Tom Love of
Publishing. Thanks go also to Richard Shellabear of Todd-White
Art Photography. I owe particular gratitude to my colleagues
Kathryn Jones and Sally Goodsir of the Works of Arts Section and
Carly Collier of the Print Room for so generously sharing their
time, knowledge and expertise. Special thanks are due to Pictures
Curatorial Intern Isabella Manning for her invaluable contribution
and to The Reverend Canon Paul Wright and to Lady Susan
Hussey for their insights. Lastly I would like to thank my family
and friends for their unfailing support and understanding.

Image rights

Published 2018 by Royal Collection Trust
York House, St James's Palace
London SW1A 1BQ

ISBN 978 1 909741 56 0
101527

British Library Cataloguing in Publication data:

A catalogue record of this book is available from the British Library

Designer Matthew Wilson
Project Manager Elizabeth Silverton
Production Manager Sarah Tucker
Editors Sarah Kane and Brian Clarke
Colour reproduction Zebra
Printed and bound in Ghent by Graphius